THE AGE OF
DINOSAURS

First published in Great Britain in 2023 by NQ Publishers,
an imprint of Nextquisite Ltd. Copyright © 2023 Nextquisite Ltd
www.nqpublishers.com

Project Director Anne McRae
Design Marco Nardi | Text Jamie Collins, Lisa Regan | Editing Susan Bishop
Layout assistant Filippo Delle Monache

Consultant Dr. Susanne Harris

ISBN 978-1-912944-81-1

Printed in China

THE AGE OF
DINOSAURS
ORIGINS DAILY LIFE EXTINCTION

NQ
PUBLISHERS

For enquiring minds

CONTENTS

6

INTRODUCTION

The dinosaurs lived for 180 million years and for most of that time they dominated life on Earth. In this book we begin by looking at their origins and how they evolved from earlier reptiles in the Triassic Period. Then we see how the real age of dinosaurs took off in the Jurassic when giant sauropods — the largest creatures ever to have walked the Earth — lived on every continent. They were hunted by some large and fearsome predatory carnivores. In the final chapters we see the huge diversity of dinosaur groups that lived during the Cretaceous. These include many of the best-known species, like T-rex and Triceratops. The period ended when the Earth was struck by an asteroid, causing a mass extinction that wiped out all the non-avian (non-bird) dinosaurs. Modern birds are the descendants of the only dinosaurs that survived.

GEOLOGICAL TIME Scientists divide the history of our planet into units of geological time. The planet formed about 4.6 billion years ago but there were no living creatures on Earth until about 540 million years ago. The first four billion years are known as the Precambrian Supereon. After that, geological time is divided into eras and periods. The dinosaurs lived in the Mesozoic Era, during the Triassic, Jurassic and Cretaceous Periods.

540
mya

299
mya

PERMIA

PALEOZOIC ERA

Prosauropods such as these Plateosaurus (see also pages 36-37) were the ancestors of later giants: the long-necked, long-tailed sauropods. Their smaller size allowed them to move around on two legs instead of four. Anchisaurus (see page 38) and Melanorosaurus (see page 44) are other examples of Triassic prosauropods.

251 mya		200 mya		146 mya		66 mya	TODAY
ERIOD	TRIASSIC PERIOD		JURASSIC PERIOD		CRETACEOUS PERIOD		

M E S O Z O I C E R A   CENOZOIC ERA

DINOSAUR EXTINCTION

THE FIRST DINOSAURS

Dinosaurs evolved from earlier reptiles during the Triassic.

They were mostly small carnivores and not main players yet.

THE GREAT DYING

A pair of fearsome male Dimetrodon reptiles prepare to fight over mating rights in what is now North America. The upright "sails" on their backs gleam in the sunshine. Behind them a huge volcano erupts, sending vast clouds of ashes and dust high into the air, blocking out the sun and foreshadowing the event known as the Permian Mass Extinction, or the "Great Dying" that would wipe out 90 per cent of life on Earth.

TYPES OF TEETH Although the sail on its back is its most striking feature, this reptile is named for its teeth. Its name means "two-measure teeth" as it had two types: serrated teeth for shearing, and sharp canine teeth for grabbing prey and ripping flesh.

Dimetrodon's sail helped with thermo-regulation. It contained blood vessels and allowed the creature to absorb heat from the sun or cool down to avoid overheating.

DIMETRODON

MASS EXTINCTIONS More than 99 per cent of life forms on Earth have become extinct. As new species evolve to fit ever changing habitats, older species fade away. But sometimes a lot of species die out over a short period of time due to faster change or even a single catastrophic event. This is known as a mass extinction.

THE GREAT DYING There have been five mass extinctions in the history of our planet. The most recent was the one at the end of the Cretaceous Period when the non-avian (non-bird) dinosaurs died out. But the largest mass extinction occurred just before the dinosaurs appeared, at the end of the Permian Period.

SAIL BACKED REPTILE Dimetrodon is not a dinosaur, even though it is often mistaken for one. It died out about 50 million years before the first dinosaurs appeared and is part of a group of reptiles known as pelycosaurs. They are more closely related to mammals than to the dinosaurs.

DIPLOCAULUS As the Dimetrodons face off, they are observed by an amphibian called a Diplocaulus. It was about about 90 cm (3 feet) long, lived in swampy areas and had an odd boomerang-shaped head.

DIPLOCAULUS

DIMETRODON (Di-MET-ro-DON)		
LIVED	290-270 mya (Permian) in North America	
FAMILY	Sphenacodontidae	
LENGTH	3.5–4.6 m (11.5–15 ft)	
WEIGHT	About 250 kg (550 lb)	
HABITAT	Dry scrubland and desert	
DIET	Carnivore: ate small amphibians and reptiles	
KEY FACTS	Four-legged, with limbs that stuck out at the sides rather than under its body	

MARSH HUNTER

A burly Batrachotomus gazes out at the shallow marshlands seeking the best place to find the fish and amphibians it feeds on. It slips into the water and quietly wades out to a likely spot to wait. Soon, with a snap of its huge jaws, it strikes, killing its prey instantly and gobbling it down in one go.

NOTABLE FEATURES Batrachotomus had a ridge of paired bony plates running along its backbone from neck to tail. It may also have had these bony plates on other parts of its body. Its long back legs and erect gait allowed it to run more quickly and efficiently than many other archosaurs.

WETLAND HABITAT Fossil remains of this creature were found in southern Germany which was a marshy wetland area during the Middle Triassic.

FISHING FOR FOOD Batrachotomus was one of the largest predators of its time, feeding mainly on fish and amphibians which it caught at the water's edge. Its teeth were sharp and curved backwards to help it keep hold of slippery prey.

BATRACHOTOMUS
(Ba-TRAK-oh-TO-mus)

LIVED	240–235 mya (Middle Triassic) in Europe (Germany)
FAMILY	Prestosuchidae
LENGTH	Up to 6 m (20 ft)
HEIGHT	Around 1.5 m (5 ft)
WEIGHT	1,100 kg (2,200 lb)
HABITAT	Wetlands with shallow pools to hunt for food
DIET	Carnivore: ate fish and amphibians
KEY FACTS	An apex predator; scaly skin especially on its back

WALKING ON ALL FOURS Unlike modern-day crocodiles, which have sprawling legs that stick out to the side, Batrachotomus walked with its legs held erect beneath its body.

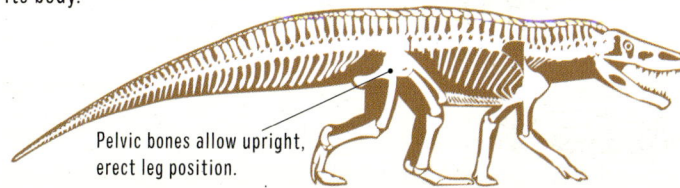

Pelvic bones allow upright, erect leg position.

Batrachotomus was not a dinosaur. It was a giant, crocodile-like archosaur, about the size of a modern saltwater crocodile. Dinosaurs were also archosaurs, but experts are not sure how closely related the two groups are.

DINOSAUR ANCESTOR Arizonasaurus was not a dinosaur; it was one of the reptiles that preceded them. The ctenosauriscidae group to which it belonged were all sail-backed archosaurs of varying sizes.

Arizonasaurus was an early archosaur, a group which includes the dinosaurs as well as birds, pterosaurs, turtles and crocodilians.

ARIZONASAURUS
(AH-ri-ZO-nuh-SORE-rus)

LIVED	240-230 mya (Middle Triassic) in the United States
FAMILY	Ctenosauriscidae
LENGTH	Around 3 m (10 ft)
HEIGHT	Up to 1 m (3.2 ft)
WEIGHT	About 225 kg (500 lb)
HABITAT	Forests and wooded areas; stayed near water where possible
DIET	Carnivore: ate small animals and fish
KEY FACTS	Thick, scaly skin to protect it from predators; walked on all fours with its dorsal spine held erect

SPEEDY PREDATOR Arizonasaurus was a dangerous predator. Its strong pelvic bones suggest it may even have been able to rise up onto its hind legs to run faster.

SAIL OR HUMP? Some scientists believe this creature had a hump rather than a sail. According to this theory, the hump was a place to store fat to be used when food was scarce.

ON THE PROWL

A ravenous Arizonasaurus scours the arid scrublands for rhyncosaurs and other reptiles to devour. It hasn't eaten in three days and is bad-tempered with hunger. Its jaws are lined with sharp teeth and when it finds a victim, it will tear it to pieces in seconds. This medium-sized cousin of the first dinosaurs has the same powerful bite of many of its meat-eating dinosaur relatives.

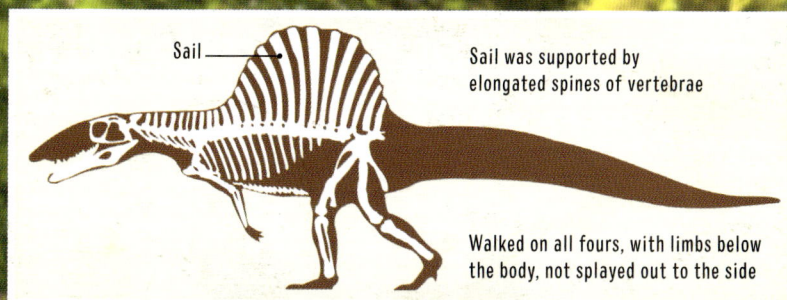

Sail

Sail was supported by elongated spines of vertebrae

Walked on all fours, with limbs below the body, not splayed out to the side

GIANT TRIASSIC REPTILES

NOT DINOSAURS Neither of these creatures is a dinosaur. Smilosuchus belonged to a group of semi-aquatic reptiles called phytosaurs. Placerias was a dicynodont, a reptilian ancestor of mammals.

Placerias are normally wary at the water's edge. They know that is where the deadly Smilosuchus lurks, waiting to ambush them as they come to drink. But today the crocodile-like Smilosuchus has eaten, so the two arch-enemies just eye each other warily and go about their business.

SMILOSUCHUS
(SMILE-oh-SOOK-us)

LIVED	228–208 mya (Late Triassic) in North America
FAMILY	Parasuchidae
LENGTH	Up to 12 m (39 ft)
WEIGHT	Up to 700 kg (1500 lb)
DIET	Carnivore: ate fish but also amphibians and other reptiles
HABITAT	Swampy land near rivers
KEY FACTS	Massive crocodile-like reptile; apex hunter; body covered in osteoderms (bony plates)

SMILOSUCHUS This giant reptile looked very like a modern crocodile. It lived in swamps and waterways where it preyed on other reptiles large and small. Its name means "chisel crocodile," and refers to the deadly, chisel-like teeth in the front of its long jaws. Despite its appearance, Smilosuchus is not closely related to today's crocodiles.

SMILOSUCHUS

BEAKY JAWS This herbivore's mouth was beak-like and tough, useful for cropping small, close-growing plants and even thicker roots and branches.

PLACERIAS (Pla-SEE-ree-as)		WEIGHT	Up to 1,800 kg (3,950 lb)
LIVED	220–215 mya (Late Triassic) in North America	HABITAT	Forests, woodlands and floodplains
FAMILY	Stahleckeriidae	DIET	Herbivore: ate roots and low-growing plants, such as ferns and mosses
LENGTH	3 m (10 ft)	KEY FACTS	Strong legs and flat, wide feet; barrel-shaped body with powerful neck and large head

HERD ANIMALS The discovery in Arizona of more than forty Placerias skeletons led scientists to believe that this animal lived in herds. The large number of fossils allowed them to carry out extensive research on how these creatures looked, moved and fed.

PLACERIAS

PLACERIAS The name means "broad body." Shaped like a hippopotamus, it was stocky and round. It may even have spent a lot of time in the water, just as hippos do today. Placerias had a short neck, barrel-shaped body, short tail and a beak-like snout with large tusk-like bones protruding from its upper jaw.

The tusks were modified front teeth

Short tail

TRIASSIC SEAS

Streamlined and sleek, this Ichthyosaur cuts through the water at top speed, changing direction with a flick of its flippers and tail. Those teeth are made for grasping, and this one has squid in its sights. Ichthyosaurs were the top marine predators for more than 150 million years.

Ichthyosaurs were unusual in that their young were born live, instead of hatching from eggs. The babies looked exactly like their parents, only smaller.

PROGANOCHELYS An early relative of the turtle, Proganochelys had teeth in the roof of its mouth. It hunted using its sense of smell, as its hearing and eyesight were not well developed. It could not pull its head into its shell, but had spines along its neck for protection.

ICHTHYOSAUR

NOTHOSAURS These large reptiles spent most of their time at sea. Their webbed feet were ideal for swimming. But their feet also had claws to help them to clamber over rocks when they came ashore.

PLACODONT

Ichthyosaur
(ICK-thee-oh-SORE)

LIVED	250–90 mya (Early Triassic to Late Cretaceous) all over the world
ORDER	Ichthyosauria
LENGTH	Up to 25 m (82 ft)
HABITAT	Shallow seas and oceans
DIET	Carnivore: fed on fish and squid-like shellfish
KEY FACTS	Shaped like large dolphins; top marine predators for most of the Mesozoic; many different species

MARINE REPTILES Prehistoric seas were awash with fascinating creatures of all shapes and sizes. Some were happy to graze on small fish and shellfish. Others were fierce hunters, the equivalent of today's sharks, seals, sea lions, dolphins and whales. They were all marine reptiles, unlike the mammals and fish that dominate modern oceans.

PLACODONTS This barrel-shaped group of reptiles liked to eat molluscs (shellfish). Their front teeth stuck out so they could dig them out of the seafloor. Their back teeth were rounded and strong, ideal for crushing shellfish.

ICHTHYOSAURS There were more than 100 species living throughout the Mesozoic. Some were small, but others were enormous. The Triassic Shonisaurus was over 25 metres (82 feet) long and was probably the largest marine reptile that ever lived.

Elongated snout

Large eye socket

Here you can see the classic Ichthyosaur shape. It looks very like a modern dolphin.

MBIRESAURUS

(Um-bee-ruh-sore-rus)

LIVED	About 235 mya (Late Triassic) in Africa
CLADE	Sauropodomorph
LENGTH	Up to 1 m (3.2 ft)
WEIGHT	9-27 kg (20-60 lb)
HABITAT	Hot but humid areas with vegetation and water
DIET	Omnivore: ate plants mostly, but also some small insects and animals
KEY FACTS	Earlist known African dinosaur; size of a chicken

EARLY AFRICAN DINOSAUR

Mbiresaurus stood barely taller than a chicken but its discovery was huge. The first dinosaurs are thought to have evolved about 235 million years ago in the southern regions of Pangaea, in what is now Africa and South America. Mbiresaurus is the oldest true dinosaur ever found in Africa.

EARLY DINOSAUR This creature was one of the very first dinosaurs on Earth. Its remains were found in 2017-2019 in Africa, in what is now Zimbabwe. They are a similar age to other early dinosaur fossils found in South America and India. At this stage of the Triassic Period, all the land on Earth was still joined together as one giant supercontinent called Pangaea. Animals were free to roam all over.

FOSSIL FINDS

Mbiresaurus walked on its back legs. Its leg bones, including a well-preserved femur and hip bone, were found as part of a nearly intact skeleton in Mbire, Zimbabwe. Only parts of its skull and one hand are missing.

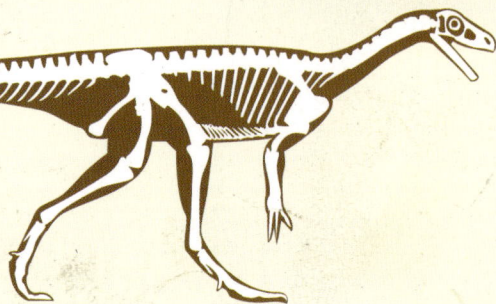

A TASTE OF THINGS TO COME The first true dinosaurs were not dominant species like their later relatives. Instead, they lived in the shadows of other reptiles such as the pseudosuchians or rauisuchians (ancient crocodile relatives) and swimming reptiles such as placodonts and ichthyosaurs. They also shared their territory with herbivores such as rhynchosaurs and cynodonts (early mammal cousins).

The oldest known dinosaur fossils date from the Middle Triassic Period (at least 235 million years ago). They are extremely rare and have been found in only a few places worldwide, mainly northern Argentina, southern Brazil, India and Africa.

DAWN RAPTORS

As the sun rises over the volcanically active river valley, a pack of wily Eoraptors comes out to forage. Standing on rocky outcrops, the dinosaurs call out to each other, and to the other animals in the

The Ischigualasto Formation where Eoraptor was discovered has been turned into a World Heritage park. It is also known as Moon Valley Park because of its striking moonlike landscapes.

EORAPTOR
(EE-oh-RAP-tor)

LIVED	About 230-223 mya (Late Triassic) in Argentina, South America
CLADE	Sauropodomorpha
LENGTH	1 m (3 ft)
WEIGHT	About 10 kg (22 lb)
HABITAT	Warm, wet river valleys with floodplains and tall forests
DIET	Omnivore or herbivore: ate plants, but may also have fed on insects and other small creatures
KEY FACTS	A very early dinosaur; bipedal, with grasping hands

A CHANGE OF TUNE

When Eoraptor was first discovered scientists believed that it was a meat-eating theropod. Later finds have made them change their minds and most experts now classify it as a plant-eating sauropodomorph.

The first Eoraptor fossils were discovered in Argentina in 1991.

ONE OF THE FIRST When Eoraptor was uncovered in the 1990s some scientists thought that it might be the first dinosaur (although others debated whether it was a dinosaur at all). Now we know of several older creatures that are unquestionably true dinosaurs (see Mbiresaurus on pages 22-23).

valley, who respond. The mix of squeaking, roaring and trumpeting may have sounded like a less melodious version of modern birds' dawn chorus.

SNOUT AND TEETH Eoraptor had a small, slender head. Its jaws were lined with two different types of teeth. At the back of its mouth it had teeth with serrated edges, which are typical of a meat-eater. But its front teeth were more leaf-shaped, like those of herbivores.

An Eoraptor skull held in an adult human's hand.

A UNIQUE FOSSIL PARK The Ischigualasto Formation in Argentina is very rich in all types of Late Triassic fossils and contains some of the oldest known dinosaur remains. Other early dinosaurs found there include Pisanosaurus and Herrerasaurus (see pages 26-27).

HOLLOW BONES Eoraptor was about the size of a fox. All of its bones were hollow, which made it light and quick on its feet. Eoraptor ran on its hind legs and used its tail for steering and balance. It had short forelimbs, or arms, ending in long fingers with sharp claws which it used to dig up roots or grasp prey.

HERRERASAURUS

Like many primitive dinosaurs, Herrerasaurus had five toes on each foot. Only the middle three supported its weight; the first and fifth toes were lost in later theropods.

AN EARLY PREDATOR Herrerasaurus was one of the first flesh-eating dinosaurs.

MEGAZOSTRODON

HERRERASAURUS
(Heh-RARE-ra-SORE-us)

LIVED	About 230 mya (Late Triassic) in South America (Argentina)
FAMILY	Herrerasauridae
LENGTH	5–6 m (16.5–19.7 ft)
WEIGHT	210–350 kg (460–770 lb)
HABITAT	Forests and woodlands, possibly also floodplains
DIET	Carnivore: ate mostly small to medium-sized reptiles and mammals
KEY FACTS	One of the earliest dinosaurs on record; lived in South America

THE FIRST MAMMALS After the Great Dying (see pages 12–13), the way was clear for new types of animals to evolve. The ancestors of modern mammals appeared in the Late Triassic and were prey for the meat-eating reptiles that roamed many parts of Pangaea. Megazostrodon (above) was one; a small, furry creature about the size of a mouse. Haramiyida (far right) was a group of rodent-like creatures, some of which may have evolved to live in trees.

MAMMALS ON THE MENU

Herrerasaurus is one of the largest early carnivores. Even so, it isn't the biggest predator in its ecosystem and doesn't go after large prey. Instead, it focuses on smaller animals. Herrerasaurus is a smart, fast predator and has no trouble finding food.

SPEEDY SPRINTER Herrerasaurus had long, muscular lower legs and short thighs and could move quickly. Its relatively long feet gave it stability. Its tail acted like a rudder for steering and balance.

DOUBLE JOINTED JAWS

Herrerasaurus had heavy jaws with serrated teeth; this shows that it was a meat-eater. Its lower jaw had a double hinge that allowed it to slide back and forth. This flexible joint helped it to clamp down on wriggling prey.

HARAMIYIDA

THRINAXODON was a mammal-like creature about the size of a fox. Its teeth suggest that it was a meat-eater. We don't know if it had fur, like modern mammals do.

Thrinaxodon fossils like this one (right) suggest that it may have hibernated in burrows like many modern mammals.

THRINAXODON

PACK HUNTERS

A lone Postosuchus struggles to defend itself against a determined group of five Coelophysis. It could easily beat off one or two of these small dinosaurs, despite their ferocity. But five together is a more difficult task. Once the larger reptile has been killed, they will eat quickly before bigger scavengers appear to steal their kill.

Pterosaurs circle above the brawl. They hope to feast on any leftovers if the Coelophysis prevail.

POSTOSUCHUS

FOSSIL REMAINS A lot of Coelophysis fossils have been found, making it one of the better known dinosaurs. A particularly rich haul came from the Ghost Ranch quarry, in New Mexico, where thousands of bones were discovered.

Coelophysis means "hollow form." It is named for its bones which are hollow.

PACK HUNTERS Coelophysis was one of the first true dinosaurs in North America. A quick and cunning carnivore, it used speed and agility to catch insects and small reptiles. Experts think that it also hunted in packs, working together to bring down larger prey, like the Postosuchus in this scene.

FAST AND LETHAL Moving on their long powerful hind legs, Coelophysis were agile and fast and could quickly cover a lot of ground in search of prey. They had razor sharp teeth and grasping hands to hold and kill their victims. They may also have hunted fish.

COELOPHYSIS

COELOPHYSIS (SEE-low-FIE-sis)	LIVED	228-201 mya (Late Triassic) in Africa and North America	HABITAT	Warm environments, such as tropical floodplains and dry deserts
	FAMILY	Coelophysidae	DIET	Carnivore: hunted insects and reptiles, may also have been a scavenger
	LENGTH	Up to about 3 m (10 ft)	KEY FACTS	Early true dinosaur; fast and lethal predator; widespread and well known
	WEIGHT	Up to about 27 kg (60 lb)		

LORDS OF THE SKIES Pterosaurs were flying reptiles, not dinosaurs. They first appeared about 220 million years ago. They are one of evolution's great success stories because they dominated the skies for more than 150 million years, before dying out at the end of the Cretaceous Period. Peteinosaurus was one of the smallest, oldest and most primitive species.

PREDATOR AND PREY All pterosaurs were agile flyers. It made them successful predators but also allowed them to evade the larger carnivores that hunted them. In the case of Peteinosaurus, this would have included Liliensternus, which also lived in Europe in the Late Triassic.

Bat-like wings

POWER STEERING
Peteinosaurus was a flyer, not a glider. Its bat-like wings propelled it high into the air for prolonged periods. Its wings were short when compared to other pterosaurs: they were only around twice the length of its back legs.

LIFE ON THE WING

When your main source of food is an aerial acrobat like the dragonfly, you need to be swift and nimble. Which exactly describes this group of Peteinosaurus, as they swoop and dive, plucking insects from the air mid-flight. Their success was short-lived though, as Peteinosaurus had become extinct by the end of the Triassic.

ON THE GROUND When they weren't in the air, these creatures rested on all fours. They moved around using both their back legs and the part of their forelimbs that look like the "elbows" of their wings.

These small pterosaurs had tiny, sharp teeth in their upper and lower jaws, ideal for grabbing insects on the wing.

PETEINOSAURUS
(Peh-TY-na-SORE-us)

LIVED	220-210 mya (Late Triassic) in southern Europe (Italy)
ORDER	Pterosauria
LENGTH	50 cm (20 in)
WINGSPAN	60 cm (2 ft)
WEIGHT	100 grams (3.5 oz)
HABITAT	Lived on the shores of the ancient Tethys Sea
DIET	Carnivore: fed on insects, such as dragonflies
KEY FACTS	One of the earliest and smallest pterosaurs; juveniles took 40 years to reach adult size

STIFF TAILS Peteinosaurus means "winged lizard." They were about the size of a large modern bat. Almost half their body length was taken up by their long, bony tails.

FACE OFF

Placerias stands its ground at the foot of this giant rock formation in what is now Arizona. Its encounter with the tiny Camposaurus shouldn't cause it any problems, but there are several of these mini-hunters, and it is blocking their route across the open scrubland. Will blood be shed, or will they pass peacefully?

HUNTER AND HUNTED Its compact size suggests that Camposaurus preyed on small creatures; probably lizards and the young of other dinosaurs. In turn, it would have been a hunted itself by bigger meat-eating reptiles.

PLACERIAS This bulky Triassic herbivore was about the size of a large modern hippopotamus. You can find more information about them on pages 18-19.

PLACERIAS

CAMPOSAURUS
(Camp-oh-SORE-us)

LIVED	227–205 mya (Late Triassic) in the United States
FAMILY	Coelophysidae
LENGTH	Unknown (too few fossils)
WEIGHT	Unknown (too few fossils)
HABITAT	Plains, with rivers and lakes
DIET	Carnivore: hunted insects, lizards and other small creatures
KEY FACTS	An early carnivore; not well known

COELOPHYSIS COUSINS Few fossils of Camposaurus have been found. Only the lower limb bones have been identified. From these, we can see it had long legs for running, and clawed, three-toed feet. They show that it was related to another more well known dinosaur, Coelophysis (see pages 28-29).

EARLY HUNTERS An animal similar to Camposaurus, called Eucoelophysis, was found nearby. At first scientists thought the two were closely related, but they now believe that Eucoelophysis was not a true dinosaur. It belonged to a sister group called silesaurids.

NEOTHEROPODS Camposaurus is one of the earliest members of a group of coelophysid dinosaurs known as neotheropods. They are the only group of theropods that survived the mass extinction at the end of the Triassic.

So few remains of Camposaurus have been found that some scientists think they shouldn't be used for analysis as they may be misleading. Even the age of the rocks where they were found is debated.

CAMPOSAURUS

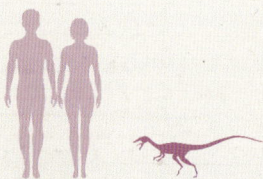

PROCOMPSOGNATHUS
(Pro-comp-SOG-nay-thus)

LIVED	220–205 mya (Late Triassic) in Europe (Germany)
FAMILY	Coelophysidae
LENGTH	Up to 1.2 m (4 ft)
HEIGHT	Up to 28 cm (11 in)
WEIGHT	About 1 kg (2.2 lb)
HABITAT	Semi-dry river valleys with volcanic activity
DIET	Carnivore: ate insects, lizards and other small prey
KEY FACTS	Not well known because of poor quality remains

COMPY

Procompsognathus was made famous by the Jurassic Park books and films, where they were known as "Compys." The film version had a venomous bite that made their victims drowsy, and were fond of eating sauropod poop. In reality, the poor quality of this dinosaur's fossils means that we don't know a lot about them.

No evidence has ever been found to support the Jurassic Park idea that Procompsognathus had a poisonous bite. None of the dinosaurs appear to have been venomous.

TINY HUNTER
Procompsognathus was a carnivore and hunted small creatures like insects and lizards. Once captured, the prey would have received a powerful bite from jaws lined with sharp, serrated teeth.

Procompsognathus may also have been a scavenger, feeding on leftovers and dead bodies.

ELEGANT JAW This dinosaur was named for its resemblance to a later dinosaur called Compsognathus (see pages 74-75). Its name means "elegant jaw." "Pro," added at the start of the name, doesn't necessarily mean it was an ancestor, only that it came before it on the dinosaur timeline.

WERE THEY EVEN DINOSAURS? While most experts think that Procompsognathus was a very early theropod dinosaur, some claim that it was a late archosaur and therefore not a dinosaur at all. The discussion will continue until better quality fossils are found.

SAFETY IN NUMBERS

A large, noisy herd of Plateosaurus ventures out of the forest to drink from the river. In the open they are vulnerable to attack by predatory dinosaurs like Liliensternus. As they pause to drink, a few individuals wait to quench their thirst. Instead, they keep watch, ready to sound the alarm if the herd is threatened by predators.

HERD LIFE Large groups of Plateosaurus skeletons have been found together in some sites. This suggests that they lived in herds, or at least gathered together in groups wherever food was plentiful. They also migrated, moving with the seasons to where food was most plentiful.

EARLY LARGE HERBIVORE
Plateosaurus was a prosauropod and an ancestor of the Jurassic sauropod giants such as Brachiosaurus. It moved on two legs or four and had a long flexible neck and a heavy tail. It was larger than other dinosaurs of its time and had thick, stocky bones.

Keen eyesight

Flexible neck

Heavy tail

STRONG HANDS Plateosaurus had powerful, grasping hands with five long fingers, or claws. The thumb claws were larger than the others and may have been used for defence as well as for collecting vegetation to eat.

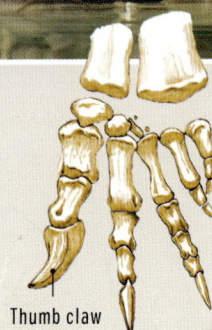

Thumb claw

FOSSILS GALORE Plateosaurus was one of the first dinosaurs to be discovered and described by scientists. Many fossils have been recovered, with over 100 skeletons found in Germany alone. Plateosaurus is one of the best known species.

PLATEOSAURUS
(Plate-ee-oh-SORE-rus)

LIVED	214-204 mya (Late Triassic) in Europe (France, Germany, Switzerland)
FAMILY	Plateosauridae
LENGTH	7-8 m (23-26 ft)
WEIGHT	Up to 4,000 kg (9,000 lb)

HABITAT	Forests near rivers and open areas where they could see predators as they approached
DIET	Herbivore: ate conifers, cycads and club ferns
KEY FACTS	One of the earliest large plant-eaters; probably lived in herds; a prosauropod ancestor of Jurassic giants like Diplodocus; large claws on each thumb

ALL MIXED UP

When the first Anchisaurus fossils were found, they were thought to be human bones. When an expert finally idenitifed it as a dinosaur, it was believed to be a meat-eating predator. Now we know that Anchisaurus is a plant-eating sauropod. This much-misunderstood creature has also gone through three name changes!

Anchisaurus often moved on all fours but could also rise up onto its back legs to walk and to reach foliage higher off the ground.

EARLY DISCOVERY Fossil remains of this dinosaur were found in 1818, and were among the first to be discovered in America. However, no one really knew what they were, and it wasn't until 1885 that it was classified as a dinosaur.

ANCHISAURUS
(ANK-ee-sore-us)

LIVED	210–190 mya (Late Triassic to Early Jurassic) in North America
FAMILY	Anchisauridae
LENGTH	1.8 m (6 ft)
WEIGHT	Up to 35 kg (77 lb)

HABITAT	Woodlands of North America
DIET	Herbivore: fed on low-growing plants and shrubs
KEY FACTS	One of the earliest dinosaurs to be discovered; long, slender body; unusual grasping hands

PLANT-EATER Anchisaurus had bigger teeth than those of related dinosaurs and its jaws were stronger, suggesting that it fed on tough food that others left untouched. It also swallowed stones, called gastroliths, to help it digest tough plant matter. It had grasping hands with claws to grab vegetation and fight off predators.

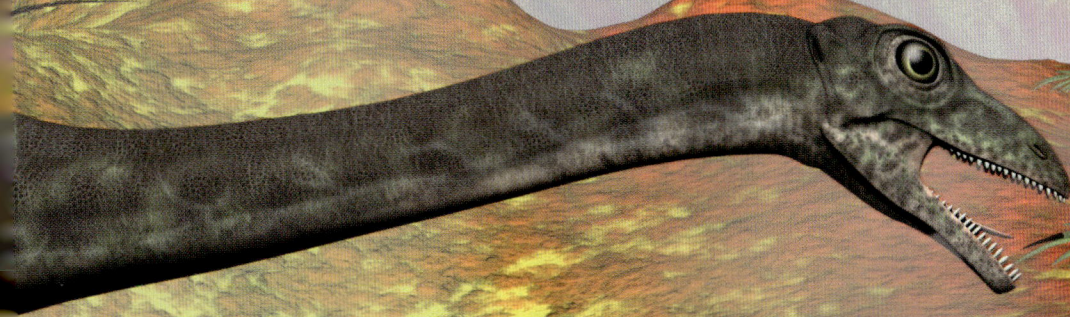

RENAMED... The naming of dinosaurs isn't always straightforward. Often, they are given a descriptive name that is later found to have been used already. In the case of Anchisaurus, this happened twice! Its previous names are Megadactylus and Amphisaurus.

... AND RECLASSIFIED
The exact classification of Anchisaurus has also caused some debate. Originally said to be a prosauropod, it is now thought to be more closely related to the sauropods.

DINOSAUR LOOKALIKES

The forest is silent and still. Suddenly, four dinosaur-like creatures scurry out of the undergrowth, splash through the stream, and are gone again. If you had been watching, you might think you had seen a group of ornithomimid (ostrich-like) dinosaurs. But this is the Late Triassic and those dinosaurs aren't due for another 80 million years. No, what you saw was a group a Effigia, a toothless reptile that looks like a six-foot-long, bipedal dinosaur, but is actually a distant cousin of modern alligators and crocodiles.

CONVERGENT EVOLUTION Sometimes animals (or plants) that live in the same habitats end up looking very similar even if they are not related. This is because they evolve in ways to best fit into their habitat. The Effigia obviously benefited from being slender, bipedal herbivores, just like the dinosaurs they resembled.

UNKNOWN DIET It is hard to be sure what Effigia ate. It had a beak but no teeth and probably cropped low-growing plants. But other animals with beaks are known to eat meat, so it is possible that Effigia did too. We need more evidence to know for sure.

ANOTHER LOOKALIKE Many of the reptiles that lived at this time looked like dinosaurs, even if they weren't. Euparkeria (below) roamed southern Africa about 245 million years ago. It looks a bit like a theropod dinosaur, but it was an archosaur ancestor and therefore a relative of the group that includes crocodilians, pterosaurs and dinosaurs.

EFFIGIA
(Ef-fij-uh)

LIVED	205 mya (Late Triassic) in North America (New Mexico)
FAMILY	Shuvosauridae
LENGTH	2 m (6.5 ft)
HEIGHT	Up to 1 m (3.25 ft)
HABITAT	Floodplains
DIET	Herbivore or omnivore: mainly ate plants and perhaps insects and other small creatures
KEY FACTS	Lightweight body, long neck and tail, large eyes and beak; bipedal

FISH FEEDER

Two hungry Eudimorphodons soar low the sea, searching for fish in the evening light. Suddenly, with its wings pressed closely against its sides, one dives headfirst into the water, reappearing a moment later with a fish flapping in its jaws. In just two quick chomps the fish is gone.

SIZE Several specimens of this creature have been found. Some are the size of a crow, while others are larger, with a wingspan up to one metre (3 feet) across.

Long stiff tail

Membrane

Elongated fourth finger

TELL TAILS
The tail of this creature had a diamond-shaped flap at the end. Like other pterosaurs, its tail was stiff and bony, and may have helped it to steer as it flew.

EUDIMORPHODON
(Yoo-die-mor-fuh-don)

WINGSPAN	Up to 1 m (3.2 ft)
HABITAT	Lake shores and coastal areas
DIET	Carnivore: mainly a fish-eater, but probably also a scavenger, like modern seabirds
LIVED	220–208 mya (Late Triassic) in Italy
FAMILY	Eudimorphodontidae
KEY FACTS	One of the earliest pterosaurs; diamond-shaped flap on tail

THECODONTOSAURUS Discovered in England, this was one of the smaller prosauropods. Its neck was relatively short and its body was about the size of a large dog. It probably ran on two legs and browsed on four.

MASSOSPONDYLUS fossils have been found in Africa and North America. It was one of the most widespread prosauropods. The first fossils were found in 1854 and many more have been uncovered since then. It grew to about six metres (20 feet) in length and had a relatively small head. It was bipedal (moved on two legs) and had grasping hands with claws for collecting food.

MASSOSPONDYLUS

ANCHISAURUS

MELANOROSAURUS
(Me-lan-or-oh-sore-us)

LIVED	227–221 mya (Late Triassic) in South Africa
FAMILY	Melanorosauridae
LENGTH	Up to 12 m (39 ft)
WEIGHT	Up to 12,000 kg (26,500 lb)
HABITAT	Warm and dry with seasonal rains
DIET	Omnivore: mostly herbivorous but may also have eaten some small animals
KEY FACTS	One of the largest of the prosauropods; moved mainly on four legs

MOUSE LIZARD Mussaurus means "mouse lizard." They got their name because the first fossils found in the 1970s were of young dinosaurs measuring 20-40 centimetres (8-16 inches) in length. They had large heads and eyes.

TRIASSIC BABIES

These hatchlings are just a few hours old. They weigh about as much as a hen's egg and would fit into the palm of your hand. They will stay together in the nest, playing and exploring their surroundings for some time, watched over by their mother. By the end of their first year, they will weigh about seven kilograms (15 pounds) and be almost independent.

FROM FOUR LEGS TO TWO Mussaurus hatchlings walked on all fours. It took them about eight years to become fully-grown adults weighing over a tonne (about the size of a modern hippopotamus). As they grew up, they changed to walking on their hind legs. Being bipedal allowed them to move and obtain food more easily.

Like human babies, these dinosaurs crawled on all fours before they learned to walk on two legs.

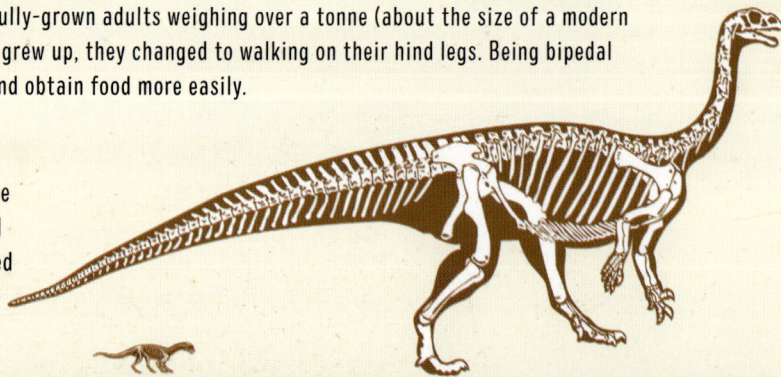

SOCIAL LIFE A Mussaurus nesting ground in Argentina contained more than 100 eggs and the skeletons of over 80 dinosaurs. The eggs, some with embryos inside, were found in clusters of 8-30, which shows they were laid in nests. The skeletons were also found in clusters, grouped by age, meaning that juveniles and adults stayed together in separate groups. This suggests that they had a social life similar to modern herd animals.

UNCERTAIN DATING The nesting site in Argentina dates to 193 million years ago. Scientists used to think this type of dinosaur lived during the Late Triassic Period, about 221-205 million years ago, whereas it now seems that they lived in the Early Jurassic.

Scientists believe that early dinosaurs like Mussaurus laid eggs with soft, leathery shells, like modern snake's eggs. Over time, most dinosaur eggs became hard, similar to present-day bird's eggs.

MUSSAURUS
(Moo-SORE-rus)

LIVED	220-190 mya (Late Triassic/Early Jurassic) in Argentina, South America
FAMILY	Mussauridae
LENGTH	Up to 8 m (26 ft)
WEIGHT	Around 1,000 kg (2,200 lb)
HABITAT	Warm, wet forest ecosystems with ferns, ginkgos, and other plant species
DIET	Herbivore: ate low-growing and medium vegetation
KEY FACTS	One of the earliest dinosaurs with proven herd and social life; juveniles moved on four legs, adults on two; laid soft leathery eggs

WIPE OUT

The Triassic Period ended about 200 million years ago in the same way that it began, with a large mass extinction wiping out up to three-quarters of life on Earth. The extinction event took place over several million years and was caused by a combination of factors, including volcanic activity, global warming and rising sea levels.

The end-Triassic extinction was one of the "big five" large-scale mass extinction events in the history of Earth.

POSTOSUCHUS

OLD PREDATORS DIE OUT Many of the top predators became extinct at the end of the Triassic. Fierce carnivores like Postosuchus and Rutiodon were not suited to the new environment and were soon replaced by an increasingly diverse number of dinosaurs.

RUTIODON

NOXIOUS GASES We still don't know what caused the end-Triassic extinction, but we do know that there was massive volcanic activity in the Atlantic Ocean at this time. This would have released huge amounts of carbon dioxide and sulphur dioxide into the atmosphere.

NEW HORIZONS The large-scale reduction of life cleared the way for new species to take over habitats that were now largely empty. The dinosaurs were the winners in this scenario, and they gradually spread and diversified to occupy and dominate all terrestrial environments, while the pterosaurs controlled the skies and marine reptiles ruled in the seas.

JURASSIC GIANTS

The real age of dinosaurs began in the Jurassic.
This was the time of the giant sauropods —
the largest creatures ever to roam
the Earth — and the carnivores
that hunted them.

The Jurassic Period was named after the Jura Mountains on the border between France and Switzerland. This was where many rocks from this period were first found and studied.

Not all Jurassic dinosaurs were giants. These early theropods were about the size of a cheetah. Their name means "dragon thief."

THE FIRST JURASSIC DINOSAUR

A fully-grown Dracoraptor runs with several juveniles as they scavenge along the shoreline. Their razor-sharp teeth are perfect for grabbing a quick bite of whatever they can find. It is much easier to feed a growing family on other predators' leftovers, but soon the youngsters will need to learn to hunt for themselves.

AN EXCITING FIND Dracoraptor found in Wales in 2014. It was an exciting discovery for scientists. It is the oldest-known specimen of a Jurassic dinosaur in the United Kingdom, and possibly in the world. It was a theropod: a fast, two-legged meat-eater and an ancestor of much bigger dinosaurs such as T-rex.

PARTIAL FIND Around 40 per cent of the skeleton was found, encased in marine rocks. It was probably washed out to sea where it sank and was scattered by fish and sea urchins that nibbled or crawled over the carcass.

JUVENILE REMAINS The fossilised bones were not fully formed and probably belonged to a young Dracoraptor. Based on its size, scientists assume that an adult would have been about three metres (9.8 feet) long.

COELOPHYSIDS Dracoraptor was an early Jurassic relative of the better known Coelophysis, with similar behaviour.

WATCH OUT! Although they were agile and quick, they were not always fast enough to stay off the menu themselves!

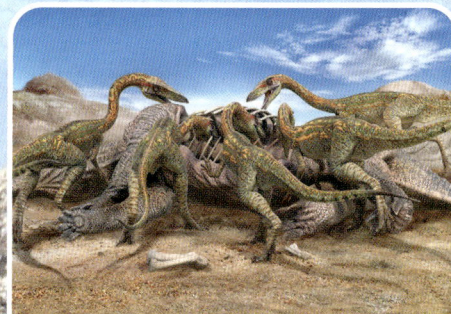

FAST FEAST After a kill, they ate quickly and moved on before larger predators and scavengers arrived and scared them off.

DRACORAPTOR
(Dray-coh-rap-tor)

LIVED	200 mya (Early Jurassic) in Wales
SUPERFAMILY	Coelophysoidea
LENGTH	Up to 3 m (9.8 ft)
HEIGHT	Up to 1 m (3.2 ft)
WEIGHT	About 30 kg (66 lb)
DIET	Carnivore: ate large insects, lizards, and other small animals
KEY FACTS	The oldest known Jurassic dinosaur in the UK; small, slender body with long tail; ran on two legs

WATCH OUT!

Keen-eyed and quick on their feet, these predatory partners are on the lookout for their next meal. At least twice the size of a modern grizzly bear, and with long tails and jaws full of sharp teeth, they are a fearsome sight. When they spot a victim, they are lightning fast.

NOT THE FILM VERSION The real life Dilophosaurus was quite different to the ones in the film Jurassic Park. They were a lot bigger, without the neck frill and they didn't spit venom.

TOP PREDATOR Dilophosaurus was one of the largest meat-eaters of the Early Jurassic in North America. It was probably a descendant of the first true dinosaurs, which evolved in South America during the Triassic. On its own, it would have hunted smaller dinosaurs and reptiles and may have caught fish. Working in packs, it would have been able to bring down some of the large sauropod dinosaurs.

KEEPING IT LIGHT Dilophosaurus bones were a bit like honeycombs; they had holes filled with air. This kept them strong and sturdy without making them too heavy.

DILOPHOSAURUS
(Die-LOAF-oh-sore-us)

LIVED	193-183 mya (Early Jurassic) in North America
FAMILY	Dilophosauridae
LENGTH	6–9 m (20–30 ft)
WEIGHT	Up to 700 kg (1,500 lb)
HABITAT	Dry, parched surroundings with seasonal sandstorms and droughts
DIET	Carnivore: ate reptiles, dinoaurs, fish
KEY FACTS	Early, large Jurassic predator; double head crest; fast powerful hunter with small forelimbs

HEAD GEAR

Dilophosaurus means "two-ridged lizard" and describes the two bony crests running from its nostrils to behind its eyes. The bone was most likely covered with keratin (the same substance as fingernails).

The head crests were made of bone, and were part of the dinosaur's skull.

The double crest was probably brightly coloured. A male with a handsome crest may have been more attractive to females at mating time.

Compared to T-rex and later apex hunters, Dilophosaurus was a medium-size predator.

AIRBORNE FISHERS

Circling the seas in search of fish, this pterosaur can see every ripple and shadow on the surface of the clear waters below. When it spies a victim, its astonishing teeth act like a basket and make quick work of scooping it up.

TWO FAMILIES The Rhamporhynchidae family had two subfamilies. One had broad snouts and short teeth. The other had longer teeth and pointier snouts. Dorygnathus belonged to the second group.

DORYGNATHUS
(DOR-e-NAY-thus)

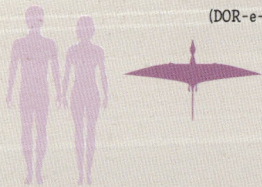

LIVED	190–182 mya (Early Jurassic) in Europe (France, Germany)
FAMILY	Rhamphorynchidae
WINGSPAN	Up to 1.5 m (5 ft)
HABITAT	Cliffs and coastlines of Europe
DIET	Carnivore: ate fish and other marine creatures
KEY FACTS	Prominent teeth in long jaws; short wings; tail with diamond-shaped fin at the end

Pterosaurs became larger and more efficient flyers as time went on.

SPLAYED TEETH Dorygnathus had long, splayed teeth at the tips of its jaws and used them to catch fish. Further back in its jaws, it had shorter teeth that were ideal for grasping onto slippery prey. Scientists have noticed wear and tear of the tooth enamel that suggests they also ate hard-shelled prey such as molluscs and crustaceans.

FOLLOW THOSE DINOS! Three Dorygnathus pterosaurs soar above a group of long-necked stegosaurid dinosaurs called Miragaia in Jurassic Portugal. The Miragaia were strict herbivores so the pterosaurs weren't looking to steal their prey. They followed the large dinosaurs as they tramped through the shallow seas because they stirred up the waters, bringing large tasty fish to the surface for them to scoop up.

ALL CLEAR!

The coast is clear – literally! Scelidosaurus may be heavily armoured but it still relies on its keen eyesight to check for danger before it leaves the safety of the forest and lumbers onto an exposed beach. It calls back to the rest of the herd to follow.

BONY BITS
The protective armour consisted of bony plates embedded in its skin. They are called osteoderms or scutes and covered its back, shoulders, sides and tail.

AMMONITES are commonly found as fossils, so we know plenty about them. Their protective shell is made up of chambers inside. The creature lived in one chamber and built new chambers to grow into.

Ammonites are cephalopods (relatives of squid and octopus). They became extinct at the end of the Cretaceous Period.

SCELIDOSAURUS
(Skel-EYE-doh-sore-us)

LIVED	201–194 mya (Early Jurassic) in England
FAMILY	Scelidosauridae
LENGTH	4 m (13 ft)
WEIGHT	About 270 kg (600 lb)
HABITAT	Forests by warm tropical seas
DIET	Herbivore: ate low-growing vegetation
KEY FACTS	Covered in armour made of bony plates; early ancestor of the ankylosaurs

Scelidosauruses lived on land, but most of their remains have been found in marine deposits. This suggests that they lived near the coast and their carcasses floated out to sea when they died.

EARLY ANCESTOR The first Scelidosaurus remains were discovered in 1858 but lay unstudied for over 100 years. We now know that this dinosaur was a primitive relative of the ankylosaurs.

AMMONITE

Elongated skull

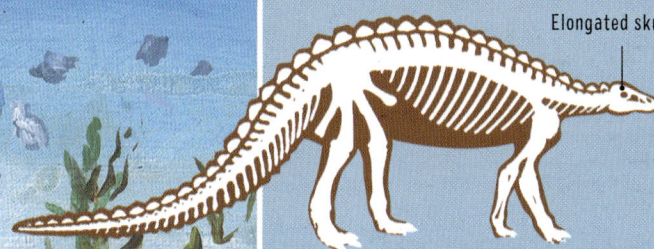

SKELETON Scelidosaurus had a long, triangular shaped skull. It had a beak for shredding leaves and small teeth in its cheeks, for crushing plants. The tail bones were joined at the back with a ball-and-socket joint that was unique to this animal. It allowed it to move freely.

TEMNODONTOSAURUS
(Tem-noe-don-toe-sore-us)

LIVED	200-170 mya (Early Jurassic) in western Europe (England, France, Luxembourg, Germany and Belgium) and Chile
FAMILY	Temnodontosauridae
LENGTH	Up to 12 m (39 ft)
WEIGHT	Up to 7,200 kg (16,000 lb)
HABITAT	Lived in the open ocean, not near the shoreline
DIET	Carnivore: apex predator of fish, plesiosaurs, ichthyosaurs and cephalopods
KEY FACTS	A type of Ichthyosaur, one of the largest; incredibly big eyes

HUGE EYES Temnodontosaurus had very large eyes. At about 40 centimetres (15 inches) across, they are among the largest eyes of any known animal. Keen eyesight made them fierce hunters.

TEMNODONTOSAURUS

JURASSIC SEAS

A shoal of prehistoric fish menaced by giant predators forms a swirling silver bait ball. In the open ocean there are no rocks or cracks to hide in, so the fish stay together in a ball for protection. Most of them will stay safe, but some unlucky ones will be gobbled up by the giant marine reptiles circling them.

MARINE REPTILES Both of the creatures seen here are marine carnivores, but from different groups. Rhomaleosaurus is a plesiosaur, with a long neck and flat tail. Temnodontosaurus is an ichthyosaur, with a pointed snout and a dolphin-shaped body.

RHOMALEOSAURUS

HUNGRY HUNTERS Rhomaleosaurus was a very large and aggressive top predator. It actively hunted small prey like fish, but also larger ones such as other plesiosaurs and ichthyosaurs. Temnodontosaurus was even bigger and was also an apex predator with a similar diet.

KEEN SENSE OF SMELL Rhomaleosaurus had a very good sense of smell. Its nostrils show that it could detect blood in the water from a distance and many other scents too. Rhomaleosaurus also had very good eyesight, so it was a well-equipped hunter.

RHOMALEOSAURUS (ROME-alley-oh-SORE-us)				
LIVED	208–175 mya (Late Triassic/Early Jurassic) in Europe (England and Germany)	HABITAT	Seas around modern-day Europe	
FAMILY	Rhomaleosauridae	DIET	Carnivore: fed on ammonites, ichthyosaurs and other plesiosaurs	
LENGTH	Up to 7 m (23 ft)	KEY FACTS	A large plesiosaur; had four big flippers to propel itself and steer in the water; very good sense of smell and eyesight	
WEIGHT	Over 2,000 kg (4,400 lb)			

Cryolophosaurus has been nicknamed "Elvisaurus" because its strange headcrest looks a bit like rock legend Elvis Presley's hairdo.

ANTARCTIC TERROR

Cryolophosaurus emits an ear-splitting, startled roar as a volcano suddenly explodes behind it, but it won't be distracted for long. Driven by a voracious appetite and an instinctive desire to track, hunt and kill, it is soon on its way. Cryolophosaurus uses its keen intelligence and powerful limbs to find and ambush prey.

HEAD CREST Cryolophosaurus had an unusual crest that ran across the top of its skull. It was probably brightly coloured and used for signalling and display during the breeding season to attract a mate.

Strange head crest

CRYOLOPHOSAURUS
(CRY-oh-lo-fuh-SORE-us)

LIVED	199–170 mya (Early Jurassic) in Antarctica
CLADE	Netheropod
LENGTH	6–8 m (19.5–26 ft)
WEIGHT	Up to 500 kg (1,100 lb)
HABITAT	Temperate forests of Antarctica
DIET	Carnivore: preyed on other dinosaurs and pterosaurs
KEY FACTS	One of the earliest meat-eating dinosaurs; bizarre crest running across the top of its head

A DIFFERENT LANDSCAPE In Jurassic times, the Antarctic was not the frozen desert it is today, but was instead covered in lush green forest. Fossilised tree trunks have been found next to Cryolophosaurus remains. It was still a long way south, and in winter the Sun barely rose above the horizon for months on end.

FEARSOME HUNTER Cryolophosaurus was one of the earliest big theropods. It had long, slender legs, grasping hands and a mouthful of sharp teeth. These had rasped edges like a saw for slicing through tough skin and flesh.

FOUR-WINGED GLIDER With several rows of long feathers on its arms and legs, Anchiornis had four wings. It also had a fringe of elongated feathers around its tail. Scientists think that all these feathers acted like a parachute as it glided from branch to branch through Jurassic forests.

BIRD-LIKE DINOSAURS

Anchiornis sits perfectly still on a branch as it keenly tracks the flight of an unsuspecting dragonfly. When the insect is within reach, it dives down on it, toothed beak agape, and snaps it up in its jaws. About the size of a modern crow, Anchiornis is remarkably bird-like in appearance, although it tends to glide rather than fly.

MULTIPLE DISCOVERIES We know more about this creature than we do about many other Jurassic animals because so many remains have been found. The first specimen was discovered in 2009 and over 200 more have been uncovered since.

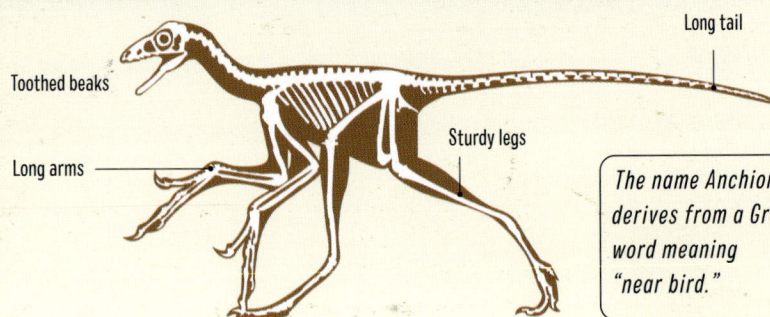

Toothed beaks

Long tail

Long arms

Sturdy legs

The name Anchiornis derives from a Greek word meaning "near bird."

BIRD-LIKE THEROPOD Anchiornis was a small theropod with long legs and tail. It also had very long arms (or wings) ending in three scaly, clawed fingers. The legs show that it was a strong runner, equally at home on the ground as it was in the trees. It is one of the earliest known gliding dinosaurs.

TRUE COLOURS

Unlike many prehistoric creatures, scientists know what colour Anchiornis was. Its fossils contained chemicals called melanosomes, which they were able to test for colour. It was black, grey and white with a rusty red crown on its head.

FUZZY AND SMALL

Clearly pursued by something scary, two tiny, bristled dinosaurs burst from the undergrowth. One has its sights clearly on the escape route in front of it, while the other takes the time to check on their pursuer behind. They need to keep their wits about them to survive.

A MIX OF TEETH These dinosaurs are members of the heterodontosaurid group that were notable for their teeth. They usually had cheek teeth, for chewing, and longer teeth near the front, including little tusks. These teeth suggest that they could eat both plants and meat.

TIANYULONG
(Tee-ang-yoo-long)

LIVED	168–151 mya (Late Jurassic) in China and Mongolia
FAMILY	Heterodontosauridae
LENGTH	Up to 1.2 m (47 in)
WEIGHT	About 5 kg (12 lb)
HABITAT	Forests, often near water
DIET	Herbivore or omnivore: ate plants and probably animals as well
KEY FACTS	Protofeathers (dino-fuzz) even though they are not theropods; mixed teeth

IMPORTANT DISCOVERY The first Tianyulong fossils were found in 2009 and they caused an uproar. Until then, scientists thought that only theropod dinosaurs had feathers (or protofeathers). Tianyulong was an ornithischian dinosaur, not a theropod. The discovery suggests that many, if not all, dinosaurs had feathers. It was an amazing find!

These peculiar dinosaurs have been described as looking like a furry parrot or a feathered cat!

A CLOSER LOOK
Tianyulong had a long row of protofeathers about 6 centimetres (2 inches) tall running all the way down its neck and back. It ran on three clawed toes. Its hands had three long fingers and two almost invisible ones.

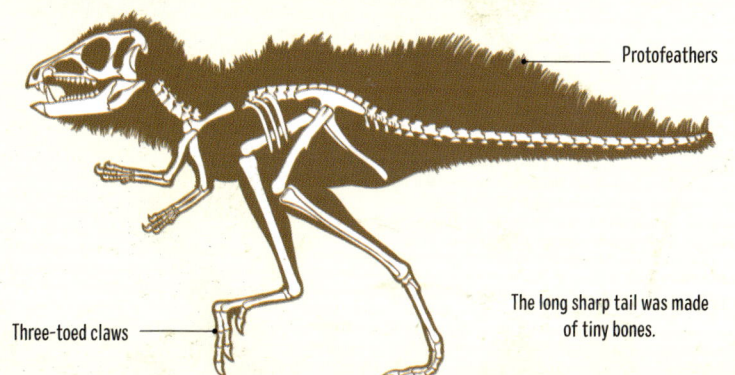

Protofeathers

Three-toed claws

The long sharp tail was made of tiny bones.

FLUFFY DINOSAURS

Two small, fluffy dinosaurs pick their way through the undergrowth in the chilly wetlands of what is now Siberia. These creatures live further north than most other dinosaurs. The climate is much colder here, but these warm-blooded little dinosaurs are kept warm by thick, downy coats of feathers.

Various skeletal remains show that Kulindadromeus had three-clawed feet and most likely walked on its toes.

RICH FINDINGS

Hundreds of Kulindadromeus fossils have been found, many of them very well preserved. It had a small snout with sharp teeth for eating plants. Its forelimbs were short but it had long legs and could run fast. Its tail was long and scaly.

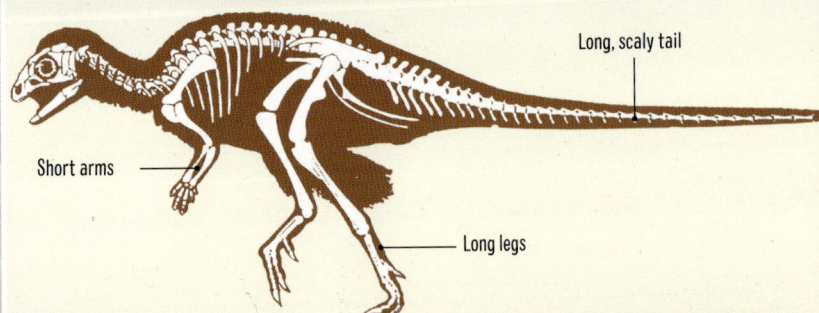

Long, scaly tail

Short arms

Long legs

WHY IS KULINDADROMEUS SO SPECIAL? Kulindadromeus was discovered in 2010, just a year after Tianyulong (see pages 66–67). Kulindadromeus was also an ornithischian dinosaur, not a theropod. The discovery backed up the earlier find and made it even clearer that many different types of dinosaurs had feathers.

KEEPING WARM Scientists think that early dinosaurs developed their feathery coats for warmth and display rather than for flight. Kulindadromeus had different types of feather-like structures on its body, from "dino-fuzz" on its trunk to longer filaments on its upper arms and legs.

KULINDADROMEUS
(Cul-lind-ah-dro-me-us)

LIVED	160 mya (Mid Jurassic) in Russia
CLADE	Neornithischia
LENGTH	1-1.5 m (3-5 ft)
WEIGHT	2 kg (4.4 lb)

HABITAT	Freshwater lake environment near active volcanoes; cool, temperate climate
DIET	Herbivore: fed on horsetails and mosses
KEY FACTS	One of the first non-theropod dinosaurs with protofeathers; lived further north than most dinosaurs

STUCK IN THE MUD

It isn't easy to move around when you weigh as much as three large elephants! Usually, Diplodocus's size is its best defence against a pack of Allosaurus, but this individual is so heavy, it has become stuck in the mud. As the predators close in, its chances of escape are slim.

> **BIG BODIES, BIG PROBLEMS** The sauropods were massive creatures. Their sheer size made it hard for their bodies to function efficiently. To carry so much weight was perhaps the most obvious problem, but it was also difficult to find enough food to sustain such a mass of flesh and to have a heart strong enough to pump blood all the way around the body.

DIPLODOCUS (Dip-LOD-uh-kus)	
LIVED	155–145 mya (Late Jurassic) in North America
FAMILY	Diplodocidae
LENGTH	25 m (82 ft)
WEIGHT	15,000 kg (33,000 lb)
HABITAT	Semi-arid plains and woodland
DIET	Herbivore: ate plants
KEY FACTS	Long neck and tail, small head

Diplodocus had a long row of spikes running along its neck and spine. They were made of keratin (like our fingernails) and could grow up to 45 centimetres (18 inches) tall.

ALLOSAURUS

DIPLODOCUS

MASSIVE LEGS AND FEET A creature of this size needed broad, flat feet to spread its weight. Each foot had five toes. The forefoot had a single large claw, while the hind foot had two claws.

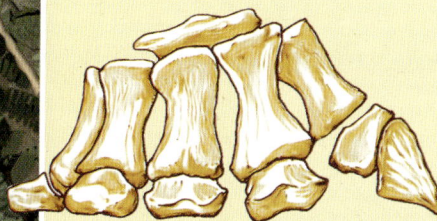

Forefoot

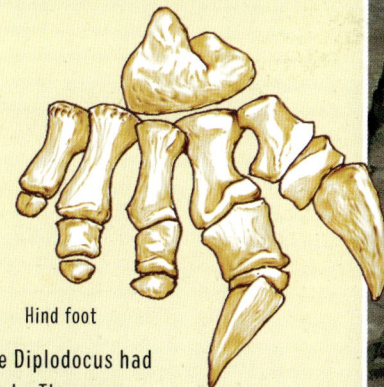

Hind foot

SOLID LIKE CULUMNS Giant sauropods like Diplodocus had four sturdy legs to support their massive body. They were strong and solid, like the columns that hold up buildings.

BABY FOOD!

A young Apatosaurus sounds the alarm to warn its brothers and sisters of impending danger. A pair of Elaphrosaurus have crept up on the unsuspecting youngsters, and they will need to shelter behind the immense body of their mother to stay safe.

HUGE SIZE Apatosaurus was so big that at first scientists thought it must have lived in the sea where the water would have helped to support its immense weight. However, studies of its bones and heart have shown that it could carry its own weight and almost certainly lived most of its life on land.

ELAPHROSAURUS

Young Apatosaurus grew quickly in their first few years. They were fully grown by the age of about ten.

SCATTERED REMAINS There are relatively few Elaphrosaurus fossils and the best examples were found in Tanzania, Africa. However, remains of similar creatures have been uncovered in other parts of Africa, in the United States, and in Australia.

MISSING SKULL No skull has been found for Elaphrosaurus. Its leg bones suggest that it was a lightweight hunter built for speed, but some more recent studies have suggested that it might have been an omnivore, or even a herbivore.

APATOSAURUS

ELAPHROSAURUS
(E-LAF-roe-SORE-us)

LIVED	157–94 mya (Late Jurassic/Early Cretaceous) in Africa (Tanzania), North America and Australia
FAMILY	Noasauridae
LENGTH	Up to 6 m (20 ft)
WEIGHT	About 200 kg (440 lb)
HABITAT	Plains, woodlands, lake shores
DIET	Carnivore, omnivore or herbivore
KEY FACTS	Long and slender, with a long neck and relatively short legs

UNLIKELY TO SURVIVE Nature was just as harsh in Jurassic times as it is today. Most of the dozen or so eggs laid by a female sauropod would be devoured by predators before hatching. Newborn hatchlings were also easy prey for a variety of predators.

APATOSAURUS
(A-PAT-uh-SORE-rus)

LIVED	161–145 mya (Late Jurassic) in North America
FAMILY	Diplodocidae
LENGTH	21 m (69 ft)
WEIGHT	24,000 kg (53,000 lb)

HABITAT	Semi-arid lands with floodplains, rivers and forests
DIET	Herbivore: ate all kinds of plants, including leaves and ferns
KEY FACTS	One of the largest land animals that ever lived

SHOWDOWN LOOMING

Three small Compsognathus dance nervously on a hillock overlooking their territory. They lash their tails in anger and let loose piercing squeals of rage. In the distance they can see two large ceratosaurs moving fast in their direction. Will they run, or stay to fight?

Compsognathus had unusually large eyes and excellent eyesight.

FEATHERS? We don't know if these small theropods had feathers. Closely related species like Sinosauropteryx in China did have feather-like skin structures, so Compsognathus may well have had them too.

Compsognathus was around the size of a modern chicken.

FAST GETAWAY Compsognathus was small but it had a long tail which it held out behind for balance and steering as it ran. It also had long, strong legs and was a fast runner.

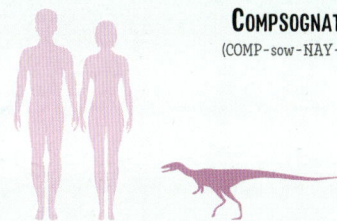

COMPSOGNATHUS
(COMP-sow-NAY-thus)

LIVED	157–145 mya (Late Jurassic) in Europe (France, Germany)
FAMILY	Compsognathidae
LENGTH	60–90 cm (2–3 ft)
HEIGHT	About 30 cm (12 in)
WEIGHT	5–6 kg (12 lb)
HABITAT	Coastal lands, islands and lagoons
DIET	Carnivore: ate lizards, small mammals, baby dinosaurs and insects
KEY FACTS	Small, lightly built and a swift runner; small front limbs

NOT THE SMALLEST For a long time scientists thought that Compsognathus was the smallest dinosaur. Now they know that there were much smaller dinosaurs; some were as tiny as modern hummingbirds!

PACK LIFE Compsognathus are often shown in packs and they may well have lived, and hunted, in groups although we have no firm evidence of this behaviour.

LONG-NECKED GIANTS

Mamenchisaurus is a gentle giant but its great size doesn't mean it is immune from attack. Its long neck and lumbering stride make it a soft target for top predators like Yangchuanosaurus. Although they are much smaller than the sauropod, working together they can weaken it enough to bring it down.

YANGCHUANOSAURUS

Yangchuanosaurus was a fierce carnivore and an apex predator in China. It was related to Allosaurus (see pages 70, 78) and similar in size, appearance and behaviour.

ADVANTAGES OF A LONG NECK This sauropod's long neck enabled it to munch the treetops that others couldn't reach. It could stand in one spot swinging its head to graze a lot of the surrounding vegetation, saving energy while taking in tons of food. The neck was also good for shedding extra body heat, like the ears of modern elephants.

YANGCHUANOSAURUS had a large head, sharp teeth and small forelimbs. It was the largest predator of the time and hunted sauropods like Mamenchisaurus and stegosaurs such as Tuojiangosaurus.

MAMENCHISAURUS

RECORD BREAKER
Mamenchisaurus had the longest neck of any known dinosaur. It was as long as its body and tail combined. The neck contained many more vertebrae than usual: 19, instead of nine or ten. They were lightweight and hollow.

Tiny head

Extremely long neck

MORE THAN ONE SPECIES Several different skeletons of Mamenchisaurus have been found, including one that is nearly complete. There are about seven species, all with huge bodies and very long necks. All the fossils have been found in China.

MAMENCHISAURUS
(Ma-MENCH-ih-SORE-us)

LIVED	160–145 mya (Late Jurassic) in China
FAMILY	Mamenchisauridae
LENGTH	22–35 m (72–115 ft)
WEIGHT	27,000 kg (60,000 lb)
HABITAT	Forests and floodplains
DIET	Herbivore: ate plants, mostly leaves from high in the treetops
KEY FACTS	Very small head on a supremely long neck; long tail

TIPPED FORWARDS Stegosaurus was fairly slow and clumsy when it walked. It moved on all fours but it had much longer hind legs than front ones. It was descended from dinosaurs that walked on their hind legs.

BONY PLATES There were more than a dozen stegosaur species living mainly in the Northern Hemisphere during the Jurassic and early Cretaceous periods. They all had rows of bony plates along their backs. Stegosaurus was one of the largest species; from head to tail it would have covered almost half a tennis court!

ALLOSAURUS

STEGOSAURUS

LEFT BEHIND

Caught alone at the back of the herd, this elderly Stegosaurus is fighting for its life. It is unable to run fast, so its only hope is to whack the Allosaurus with a powerful enough blow of its spiked tail to offset the attack. On this occasion the Stegosaurus wins and the Allosaurus backs off, but things don't always go this well.

The four-spiked tail is known as a thagomizer. Each spike could be as long as a baseball bat.

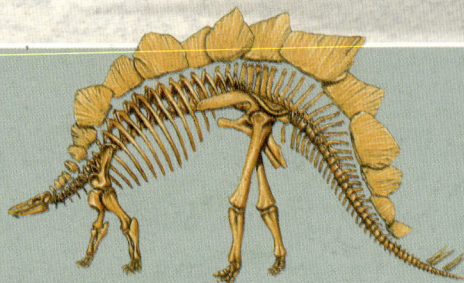

PEA BRAINS Although Stegosaurus was enormous, its skull was very small and its brain was tiny (about half the size of a sheep's brain).

SPIKED TAIL The back plates may have warned a predator to stay away, but the tail spikes were its real defence. Stegosaurus swung its tail like a weapon. Allosaurus fossils show holes made by these tail spikes.

Thagomizer

The plates along a Stegosaur's back were made of bone but they were not attached to the spine.

STEGOSAURUS
(STEG-oh-SORE-us)

LIVED	156–145 mya (Late Jurassic) in North America and Europe (Portugal)
FAMILY	Stegosaurinae
LENGTH	Up to 10 m (32.8 ft)
WEIGHT	About 1,600 kg (3,500 lb)

HABITAT	Open forests and semi-arid floodplains
DIET	Herbivore: ate mosses, ferns, horsetails, cycads and conifers
KEY FACTS	Large, bulky body which stood on four straight, pillar-like legs; bony plates and spiked tail

SNAPPY HUNTERS

It takes keen reflexes and lightning speed to capture insects on the wing, but that's not a problem for these juvenile Ornitholestes. Their sharp eyesight allows them to track giant dragonflies and snap them out of the air to enjoy as a crunchy snack.

GRABBY HANDS Ornitholestes had long arms with clawed fingers on the end of its hands. Its mouth was fairly small, so it probably grabbed prey with both hands, holding onto it while delivering a killer bite.

Ornitholestes used its long grabby hands to capture prey.

SCARCE REMAINS Most of what we know about Ornitholestes comes from one partial skeleton. It was found in the Morrison Formation in the United States. This rock formation is famous for the many different dinosaur fossils found there. See pages 88-89 for more information.

FAULTY FOSSILS Ornitholestes is usually shown with a small crest on its snout. However, we can't be sure that this is how it looked. The "crest" may have been a piece of skull that was pushed out of place during the fossilisation process.

AGILE PREDATOR

Ornitholestes means "bird robber" and these fox-sized predators may have hunted birds as well as lizards, frogs early mammals and hatchling dinosaurs. Packs of Ornitholestes working together may have hunted larger prey.

ORNITHOLESTES
(Or-nith-oh-LESS-teez)

LIVED	155–145 mya (Late Jurassic) in the US
FAMILY	Coeluridae (debated)
LENGTH	Around 2 m (6.5 ft)
WEIGHT	About 12–15 kg (26–33 lb)
HABITAT	Forests of western North America
DIET	Carnivore: ate insects, lizards, frogs, early mammals and other small dinosaurs
FEATURES	Fox-sized but with slender legs and arms; walked on hind legs

FAMILY GATHERING

An adult Brachiosaurus pounds its giant foot in warning to protect its offspring as they drink at the river. Most creatures know to keep a safe distance from a fully grown Brachiosaurus; these huge animals are far too large to attack. But the crocodile-like creature lurking in the shallows clearly thinks that a baby Brachiosaurus might make a tasty snack!

In contrast to creatures such as Stegosaurus, Brachiosaurus had forelegs that were longer than its hind legs. These helped to raise the front of its body to feed from the treetops.

FIRST CROCODILES The earliest ancestors of modern crocodiles evolved around 200 million years ago during the Early Jurassic. There were many different types, some of which were meat-eaters that lived mainly in the water like modern species. But there were others that lived on land, and some that were herbivores.

HIGH BROWSERS Around half of Brachiosaurus's height came from its neck. Its neck bones were 30 times longer than a human's, measuring up to one metre (3.2 feet) each. It could nibble on leaves the height of a four-storey building. These huge creatures ate about 200 kg (440 pounds) of vegetation every day.

Brachiosaurus was one of the tallest dinosaurs; it was about two and a half times as tall as a modern giraffe.

BRACHIOSAURUS
(Brak-ee-uh-SORE-us)

LIVED	155–140 mya (Late Jurassic) in North America, Portugal, Tanzania and Algeria	
FAMILY	Brachiosauridae	
LENGTH	Up to 30 m (98 ft)	
WEIGHT	Up to 45,000 kg (99,000 lb)	

HEIGHT	Up to 15 m (49 ft)
HABITAT	Semi-arid regions, with extremes between wet and dry seasons
DIET	Herbivore: ate ferns, ginkos and conifers
KEY FACTS	One of the tallest dinosaurs; very long, sturdy neck; small skull

LOOK OUT!

An Iguanodon mother is startled by the sudden appearance of a fierce Megalosaurus. She is not afraid for herself. She has a massive body and dangerous thumb spikes that would make any but the largest predators think twice about attacking her. But she has two babies with her and they are tempting morsels for this vicious carnivore.

TREACHEROUS LANDS Iguanodons lived in marshy areas full of treacherous quicksands and predatory reptiles, including crocodiles and meat-eating dinosaurs. Young, old and sick individuals were easy prey.

IGUANODON

EARLY DISCOVERY Iguanodons were one of the first dinosaurs discovered. Fossil collector Mary Mantell first found their teeth in 1822. They lived over a large area and many fossils have been found. They are one of the best known species.

HAND SPIKES Iguanodon had 30-centimetre (12-inch) long spikes on its hands instead of thumbs. They may have been used for defence or to help gather food. When Iguanodons were first discovered, scientists thought the spikes were horns that grew on their noses!

THUMB SPIKES

We don't know for sure what the spike was for.

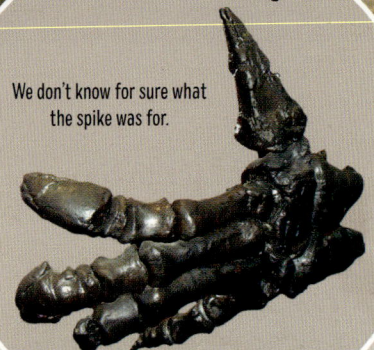

MEGALOSAURUS

GENTLE PLANT EATERS Iguanodons were herbivores. They had long narrow skulls with a large beak for cropping foliage from trees. Behind the beak, lay at least 100 teeth which were used to grind up the tough plant fibres. They were one of the first species of dinosaurs to have teeth for pulping food in their mouths.

IGUANODON (Ig-WAH-no-don)	LIVED	160-94 mya (Late Jurassic-Early Cretaceous) in Europe, North America and Asia	WEIGHT	4,500 kg (10,000 lb)
	FAMILY	Iguanodontidae	HABITAT	Forests, coastal inlets, swamplands and islands
	LENGTH	9-11 m (20-30 ft)	DIET	Herbivore: fed on all types of plants
	HEIGHT	Up to 3 m (10 ft)	KEY FACTS	Massive herbivore; lived in herds; one of the first dinosaurs discovered

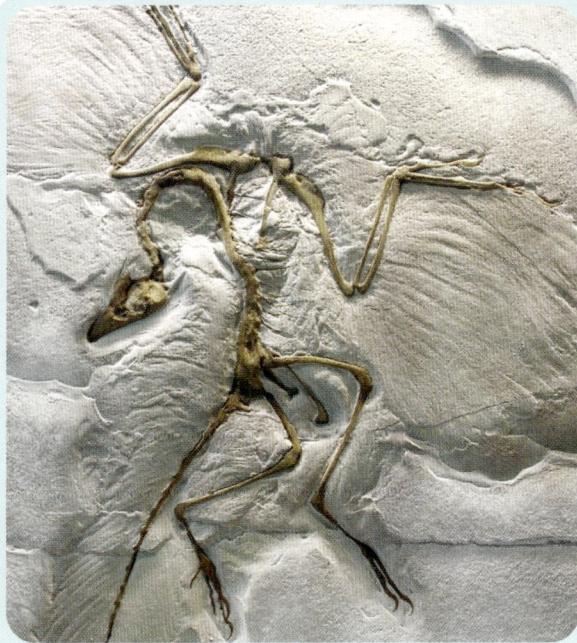

EVOLUTION The first complete Archaeopteryx fossil was found in 1861, just two years after Charles Darwin published his groundbreaking treatise on evolution, *On the Origin of Species* (1859). This fossil, which apparently showed a dinosaur that was transforming into a bird, seemed to perfectly illustrate Darwin's ideas about how a species could gradually change into an entirely new one.

ARCHAEOPTERYX
(ARK-ee-OP-tur-iks)

LIVED	150–147 mya (Late Jurassic) in Europe (Germany)
FAMILY	Archaeopterygidae
LENGTH	50 cm (20 in)
WEIGHT	0.5–1 kg (1.1–2.2 lb)

HABITAT	Coastal lands, islands and lagoons
DIET	Carnivore: fed on insects, small mammals and reptiles
KEY FACTS	One of the most important fossils ever found, it shows that birds evolved from dinosaurs

THE FIRST BIRD

An Archaeopteryx perches on the branches of a low-growing tree, ready to stretch its wings and take off. It can fly over short distances and glides easily from branch to branch in the forests. About the size of a raven, it looks very like a modern bird, although it has a mouth full of teeth.

Archaeopteryx was about the same size as a modern magpie. It had feathers, sharp teeth and a long bony tail.

HALF BIRD, HALF DINOSAUR
Palaeontologists now agree that dinosaurs are the ancestors of modern birds, but the idea was hotly debated for more than 150 years. The debate was set off by the discovery of several well-preserved fossilised skeletons of Archaeopteryx, a creature that seemed to be half bird, half dinosaur.

If you compare the skeleton of a modern bird with that of a theropod dinosaur, you can see just how similar they are. The dinosaurs had long bony tails, which birds have lost, but they both walk on their hind legs, have flexible necks and large eyes. They also share some more complex anatomical similarities.

Skeleton of a theropod dinosaur

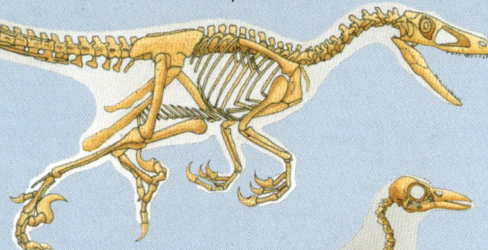

Skeleton of a modern bird

A STUNNING FIND Archaeopteryx was found in a limestone quarry in Bavaria, Germany. Its discovery made scientists realise that some dinosaurs, especially the theropods, shared many characteristics with modern birds, including light, hollow bones and a covering of feathers.

MARCHING TO THE CRETACEOUS

By the end of the Jurassic Period the supercontinent Pangaea had split apart into two smaller land masses called Laurasia (in the north), and Gondwana (in the south).

WHAT LIVED THERE? The Morrison Formation was home to sauropods such as Diplodocus, Barosaurus, Brontosaurus, Apatosaurus, and Camarasaurus. It also had smaller plant-eaters such as Stegosaurus, Dryosaurus and Camptosaurus. Allosaurus hunted here, as did Ceratosaurus and Dilophosaurus.

Changes in climate and the environment led to the extinction of many of the Jurassic sauropods and stegosaurs. New species – such as the ceratopsids, spinosaurids and coelurosaurs – appeared and diversified. By the Early Cretaceous, the stage was set for the greatest period in dinosaur history.

THE GOLDEN AGE

The Cretaceous was the Golden Age of Dinosaurs.

They dominated life on every continent.

LETHAL CLAWS

Sickle-shaped sharp claw

Deinonychus means "terrible claw," and refers to the big, sickle-shaped claws on the raptors' hind limbs. A single, well-aimed kick with one of these could slash and kill a victim. When not in use, the claw was held up off the ground so that it didn't get blunt.

LETHAL HUNTERS

A bloodthirsty pack of Deinonychus descends upon two hulking Ankylosaurs. Normally these mid-size predators would not be able to bring down such large herbivores, but one of the two Anklyosaurs is old and sick and will be unable to defend itself from the vicious predators. They will score an excellent meal!

CO-OPERATIVE PREDATORS
Deinonychus was not a particularly large dinosaur and scientists think that they may have hunted together in packs to bring down prey much larger than themselves.

STIFF TAILS Like all raptors, iDeinonychus had a series of ossified (bony) tendons in its tail that made it quite rigid. It probably used the tail like a rudder for steering and balance while running.

JURASSIC PARK The deadly Velociraptors in Steven Spielberg's films are actually based on the size, proportions and snout shape of Deinonychus. Velociraptors were much smaller than Deinonychus and they lived in Asia, not North America. See pages 114-115 for more on Velociraptors.

BIRD-LIKE RAPTORS The body shape and bones of a Deinonychus were a lot like those of modern birds. Scientists think that, like many dromeosaurs, Deinonychus was covered in feathers, although no solid proof of this has been found.

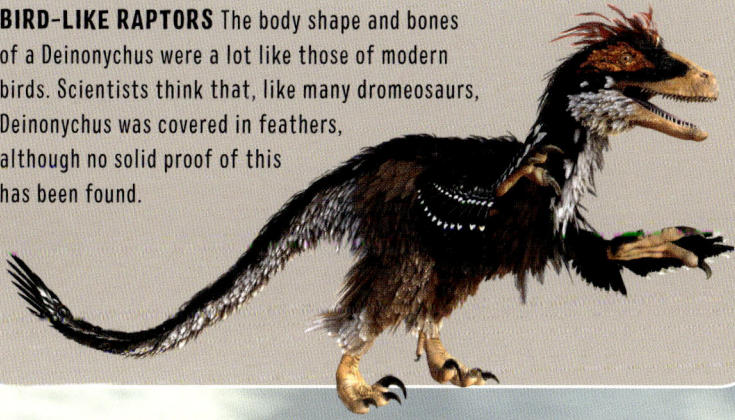

DEINONYCHUS (Dye-NON-ee-cuss)	**LIVED**	125-100 mya (Early Cretaceous) in western North America
	FAMILY	Dromeosauridae
	LENGTH	Up to 3.4 m (11 ft)
	WEIGHT	Up to 100 kg (220 lb)

HABITAT	Floodplains, close to woodlands where herbivorous dinosaurs grazed
DIET	Carnivore: preyed on other dinosaurs, early mammals and anything else it could catch
KEY FACTS	Intelligent, agile, vicious; armed with lethal curved claws on hind feet

LAKESIDE LIVING

A family group of Caudipteryx spend their days on the lakeshore. They pull up plants and swallow them down without chewing. Caudipteryx is quick on its feet and also catches insects, small fish and aquatic creatures.

FEATHERED AND BIRD-LIKE Caudipteryx was one of the first feathered dinosaurs to be found. Their discovery in the 1990s caused intense debate. Some scientists claimed that it wasn't a dinosaur at all, but an early bird. Today, most agree that it is a dinosaur and that it proves that birds evolved from dinosaurs.

SPECTACULAR TAIL FEATHERS Caudipteryx had a short, stiff tail with a fan of long feathers on its tip. None of Caudipteryx's feathers are suitable for flight and they were probably used for display (to attract a mate) and warmth.

BIRD HEAD
Caudipteryx had large eyes and keen eyesight. It had only a few teeth in the front of its upper jaw. The snout looked very much like a modern bird's beak. Since it couldn't chew its food, it swallowed small stones that stayed in its gut to help grind everything up.

FROGS AND TURTLES
Frogs evolved about 250 million years ago, well before the dinosaurs. Turtles, like the one on the tree trunk on the facing page, first appeared even earlier, about 260 million years ago.

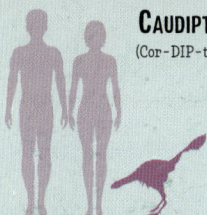

CAUDIPTERYX
(Cor-DIP-ter-iks)

LIVED	125–120 mya (Early Cretaceous) in China
FAMILY	Caudipteridae
LENGTH	Up to 1 m (3.3 ft)
WEIGHT	About 2 kg (4.4 lb)

HABITAT	Subtropical forests and wetlands
DIET	Omnivore: fed on plants, insects, small fish and invertebrates
KEY FACTS	Long legs and short arms; covered in feathers; spectacular long tail feathers; could not fly

ANCIENT HORNED FACE

The silence of the rocky landscape is pierced by the screams of two male Archaeoceratops as they face off in a furious battle over mating rights. These primitive ceratopsids are about the size of a cocker spaniel and — unlike their hulking descendants — they can move swiftly on their hind legs.

ANCESTOR OF TRICERATOPS It's hard to believe that tiny Archeoceratops, or "ancient horned face," is the ancestor of the massive, fancy-frilled ceratopsids like Triceratops that roamed North America in the Late Cretaceous. It is just one of many small ceratopsid dinosaurs that have been discovered in Asia.

VEGETARIAN DIET Like all ceratopsids, Archaeoceratops was herbivorous. It lived in the Early Cretaceous before grasses had evolved and fed on low-growing ferns, cycads and conifers. It used its sharp beak to bite off the tough plants them chomped them into pieces to swallow.

ASIAN ORIGINS All of the early ceratopsid dinosaurs discovered so far lived in China and Mongolia. This suggests that the family originated in Asia during the Late Jurassic and spread from there to North America and Europe.

HUGE HEAD
Archaeoceratops had a very large head compared to its body. Despite its name, it had no horns on its face and just one small bony frill lining the back of its head.

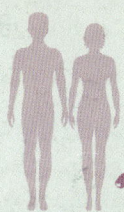

ARCHAEOCERATOPS
(AR-kay-oh-SEH-rah-tops)

LIVED	129–100 mya (Early Cretaceous) in China and Mongolia
FAMILY	Archeoceratopsidae
LENGTH	Up to 1.30 m (4.3 ft)
WEIGHT	About 85 kg (187 lb)

HABITAT	Rocky landscapes, with low-growing ferns, bushes and tall trees
DIET	Herbivore: ate ferns, cycads and conifers
KEY FACTS	Early ceratopsid, ancestor of Triceratops; size of a cocker spaniel; very large head

PINT-SIZE PREDATORS

The two tiny raptors have been hunting all day in the trees, going after the small birds and reptiles they love to eat. In the early evening they glide down to the lake to drink and cool off in the shallows. Later, they will flap their way back up to the treetops and snuggle together to stay warm as they sleep.

ON THE GROUND It was not easy for Microraptors to move on the ground due to their wings and the long feathers on their arms and legs. Even folded, the wings would have dragged along in the mud. This is why scientists think that Microraptors probably spent most of their time in the trees.

FEEDING Some fossils of Microraptor guts contain the remains of their last meal. This is how we know that they ate small mammals, birds and fish. They were active hunters and scavengers.

MICRORAPTOR
(MY-crow-rap-tor)

LIVED	125-112 mya (Early Cretaceous) in China and Mongolia
FAMILY	Anchionithidae
WINGSPAN	1 m (3.2 ft)
WEIGHT	Up to 1 kg (2.2 lb)
HABITAT	Forests
DIET	Carnivore: fed on a variety of mammals, birds, fish and lizards
KEY FACTS	Small predators; four wings

FOUR WINGS About the size of pigeons, Microraptors were tiny compared to most other dinosaurs. They had four wings with long feathers on their arms and legs. Scientists think that they were skilled gliders but probably not strong, true fliers. They would have struggled a little with powered flight.

PHENOMENAL FOSSILS IN LIAONING Like many other small, feathered dinosaurs, Microraptor was first discovered in a region of northeastern China called Liaoning. From the mid 1990s, sensational finds here proved that dinosaurs were the ancestors of modern birds, resolving a long-running scientific dispute.

STEALTHY HUNTERS

A pair of very large Suchomimus slip quietly into the warm, softly flowing waters of the delta, barely making a sound as they paddle out to the depths. They know that this is the time of year that plump garfish return upstream to spawn, and they are ready for them. Suddenly, one of them dives down and grabs a fish in its jaws. It's pandemonium as blood fills the water and the fish panic, trying to escape. But now the other Suchomimus is diving and it is just too late for six of the largest fish!

SUCHOMIMUS
(SOO-ko-MIME-us)

LIVED	120–110 mya (Mid-Cretaceous) in Africa
FAMILY	Spinosauridae
LENGTH	Up to 12 m (40 ft)
WEIGHT	Up to 6,000 kg (13,000 lb)
HABITAT	Floodplains near rivers and lakes
DIET	Carnivore: mainly ate fish and marine reptiles, but was also a scavenger
KEY FACTS	Elongated, toothy snout; strong swimmer, hunted mainly in the water

Suchomimus was discovered in Niger, in Africa, in 1997. Its long curved claws and stabbing thumb spike were ideal for fishing.

CROCODILE-LIKE Suchomimus means "crocodile mimic" and these large predators are aptly named. Their elongated, skinny snouts were lined with teeth that were designed to catch slippery fish. They had long, powerful arms with three-clawed hands to grab and hold fish.

SPINOSAURUS COUSIN Suchomimus was related to Spinosaurus (see pages 100–109), although it did not have a tall sail on its back like its larger cousin. Suchomimus lived just before Spinosaurus.

POWERFUL JAWS Giganotosaurus had 76 teeth lining it jaws and each tooth was 20 cm (8 inches) long. Although its skull was larger than that of T-rex, it seems to have had less "bite power" than its later North American cousin. Giganotosaurus had a brain about the size of a banana (smaller than T-rex).

DESPERATE MEASURES

Three hulking Argentinosaurus bellow in fear and rage as a hungry Giganotosaurus closes in. Although bigger than T-rex, the mighty predator would not normally attack titanosaurs on its own. But the dinosaurs' homelands are living through the longest drought the region has ever known and our Giganotosaurus is starving. Will it suceed?

GIGANOTOSAURUS
(Gig-AN-oh-toe-SORE-us)

LIVED	100-93.5 mya (Late Cretaceous) in South America (Argentina)
FAMILY	Carcharodontosauridae
LENGTH	Up to 13 m (43 ft)
WEIGHT	Up to 13,800 kg (30,500 lb)
HABITAT	Plains and woodlands
DIET	Carnivore: fed on other animals, including dinosaurs
KEY FACTS	Big, strong and fast; short arms with 3 sharp claws; thin, pointed tail for balance and agility

BIGGEST SOUTH AMERICAN CARNIVORE Giganotosaurus roamed the plains and forests of South America about 30 million years before Tyrannosaurs rex lived in North America. It was alive at the same time as the Spinosaurus, the largest meat-eating dinosaur of all time, which lived in what is now North Africa (see pages 108-109).

ARGENTINOSAURUS
(AR-jen-teen-oh-SORE-us)

LIVED	99-89 mya (Late Cretaceous) in South America
GROUP	Titanosauridae
LENGTH	Up to 40 m (130 ft)
WEIGHT	Up to 11,000 kg (22,000 lb)
HABITAT	Forests and plains
DIET	Herbivore: fed on upper branches of tall trees
KEY FACTS	Slow-moving and very large; juveniles took 40 years to reach adult size

WORLD'S BIGGEST DINOSAUR According to many, Argentinosaurs was the largest dinosaur that ever walked the Earth. Argentinosaurus females laid 10–15 eggs at a time; the eggs measured about 30 cm (1 foot) in diameter and are among the largest dinosaur eggs on record.

AN EASY MEAL

The stagnant waters in the lagoon have killed off lots of giant shrimp. The young Scipionyx crunches through their shells to get at the delicious flesh within. It keeps a keen eye out for the fearsome crocodiles that infest the tepid waters.

ISLAND DWELLER Scipionyx lived on an island in the Tethys Sea between Laurasia and Gondwana, in an area that is now part of the Mediterranean Sea. The early Cretaceous waters were often low in oxygen, very salty and filled with toxic algae.

JUST ONE FOSSIL
Everything we know about this dinosaur is based on one remarkable fossil of a three-day-old hatchling. Not only was the skeleton almost complete, it also contained soft tissues, such as parts of the digestive system, liver, blood vessels and muscle. Scientists even found the remains of its last meal — fish and lizards.

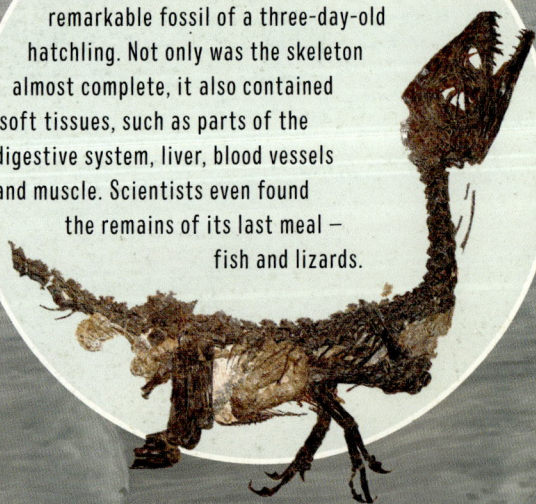

AN IMPORTANT FOSSIL Scipionyx is one of the most important fossils ever found. It is unique because so many of the dinosaur's internal organs were preserved. Scientists think it drowned in an oxygen-poor lagoon, which helped to protect these body parts.

TURBO-CHARGED! Scientists describe Scipionyx as turbo-charged. This relatively small predator was capable of intense bursts of speed and would have been able to hunt down the smaller reptiles in its habitat and catch fish in the shallows.

Scipionyx had large eyes and excellent eyesight. It was an unusually intelligent dinosaur. Its only enemies were the short-muzzled crocodiles that also lived on these islands.

Scipionyx may have been covered in an early form of feathers but none of the skin was preserved so we don't know for sure.

SCIPIONYX
(SHIH-pee-OH-niks)

LIVED	113–109 mya (Early Cretaceous) in Italy
FAMILY	Compsognathidae
LENGTH	2 m (6.6 ft)
WEIGHT	25–30 kg (55–66 lb)

HABITAT	Beaches, salt marshes, lagoons
DIET	Carnivore: hunted fish, lizards, small vertebrates; also scavenged
KEY FACTS	Swift, deadly hunter, small arms, big tail; walked on its hind legs; big head and sharp teeth

THE BATTLE FOR THE SKIES

A pterosaur catches a fish and heads to the rocky shoreline to enjoy its meal in peace. Suddenly, it is set upon by a rowdy bunch of Ichthyornis. They squawk and screech, all the while dive-bombing its mouth, trying to prise the fish loose. To get free of them, the pterosaur tosses the fish back into its gullet, swallowing it in a single gulp.

GONE WITH THE DINOSAURS Ichthyornis died out when the asteroid hit at the end of the Cretaceous, along with all the other species of toothed birds. Only the toothless ancestors of modern birds survived.

A hungry Ichthyornis tugs greedily at the fish in the pterosaur's beak.

PTEROSAURS AND BIRDS Pterosaurs evolved before birds and they ruled the skies throughout the Mesozoic Era. The first birds appeared about 150 million years ago, and by the early Cretaceous a wide variety of them shared the skies with pterosaurs. In some places they competed for resources, but the pterosaurs kept the upper hand because they were so much larger. Birds could only really compete in areas where their small body size and agility were advantageous.

TOOTHY SEABIRDS Ichthyornis was a seabird about the size of a pigeon. It was a strong flyer and looked quite similar to a modern bird, except that it had a full set of sharp, curved teeth. The first fossils were discovered in 1870, but the skullls were not in good shape. Only more recent finds revealed that they had teeth.

Ichthyornis had a powerful jaw and bite. In this respect it was much more like a dinosaur then a modern bird.

ICHTHYORNIS
(Ik-fee-or-niss)

LIVED	99-70 mya (Late Cretaceous) in North America
FAMILY	Ichthyornithidae
WINGSPAN	Up to 60 cm (23.6 in)
WEIGHT	About 25 kg (55 lb)
HABITAT	Lived along the coastline of the shallow waters of the Western Interior Seaway
DIET	Carnivore: ate fish
KEY FACTS	Very like a modern bird, except for teeth; died out with the dinosaurs

FISH DINNER!

Spinosaurus wades into the rushing waters and waits. It knows that sooner or later an unsuspecting fish will swim by. Here it comes! It's an Onchopristis (giant sawfish). Spinosaurus plunges its long crocodile-like snout into the water and hauls the giant fish out by its tail. It gives the fish a few shakes to stun it then flings it onto the bank. A good fish dinner!

THE BIGGEST CARNIVORE Recent research shows that Spinosaurus was the largest of all the meat-eating dinosaurs, bigger even than T-rex. With its tall sail soaring above its back, it was an impressive creature.

SPINOSAURUS
(SPINE-oh-SORE-us)

LIVED	112–93.5 mya (Late Cretaceous) in North Africa
FAMILY	Spinosauridae
LENGTH	Up to 18 m (59 ft)
WEIGHT	Up to 21,000 kg (46,000 lb)
HABITAT	Tidal flats, mangrove forests, swamps
DIET	Carnivore: ate fish, lizards, turtles
KEY FACTS	Very large; tall sail along its back; elongated crocodile-like snout; first dinosaur known to swim

SAILING ALONG Spinosaurus had 1.65-metre (5.5-foot) tall vertebrae along its back. They were covered with skin and looked like a tall sail. Scientists think that the dinosaur may have used the sail to regulate its body temperature, or to impress rivals and potential mates during courtship displays.

SOARING GIANTS

A small flock of pteranodons skims along the surface of the sea almost without flapping their wings as they grab fish in their long beaks. They use the air currents to hunt, just as albatrosses do today. They don't spend much time on sea or land, preferring to spend most of their lives gliding and soaring in the air above the ocean.

A WIDELY KNOWN PTEROSAUR
More than 1,200 fossil remains of Pteranodon have been found, making it one of the best known pterosaurs. The first fossils were discovered in 1871. They were among the earliest pterosaurs to be found outside Europe. Up until the late 20th century when they were eclipsed by the vast Quetzalcoatlus (see page 124), they were also believed to be the largest.

TOOTHLESS Pteranodon's name means "wings and no teeth." Unlike earlier pterosaurs such as Peteinosaurs (see pages 30-31) and Dorygnathus (see pages 56-57), they had toothless beaks, like those of modern birds.

There were two types of Pteranodons. They were quite similar, except for the shape of their head crests.

Pteranodons did spend some time on land. Scientists disagree on how they walked. Some think that they moved on all fours.

Other experts believe that they walked along on their hind legs, keeping their forelimbs and wings off the ground.

This is a Pteranodon sternbergi. It had an upright crest, unlike the other species, known as Pteranodon longiceps, which had a long, backward-pointing crest.

Pteranodon fossils have been found in the area that was submerged by the ancient sea known as the Western Interior Seaway. It divided North America into eastern and western parts during the Late Cretaceous.

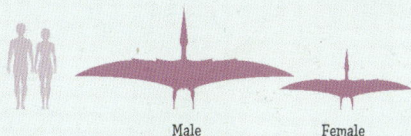

PTERANODON
(Teh-RAN-oh-don)

Male

Female

LIVED	90-70 mya (Late Cretaceous) in North America
FAMILY	Pteranodontidae
WINGSPAN	Up to 6 m (20 ft)
LENGTH	1.5-2 m (5-6.5 ft)
WEIGHT	20-50 kg (44-110 lb)
HABITAT	Coastlines and shallow inland seas of the Western Interior Seaway
DIET	Carnivore: mainly ate fish
KEY FACTS	Massive size; large skull crest; toothless beak

MAIASAURA
(MY-ah-SORE-a)

LENGTH	Up to 9 m (30 ft)
WEIGHT	Up to 2,500 kg (5,500 lb)
HABITAT	Inland, in green areas and forests
DIET	Herbivore: ate leaves, berries, seeds and woody plants
KEY FACTS	Nested in colonies; walked on all fours, large but could move at 40 km/h (25 mph)

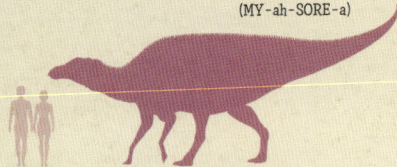

LIVED   86–70 mya (Late Cretaceous) in North America

FAMILY   Hadrosauridae

GOOD MOTHERS

It is early morning in the nesting colony and the Maiasura mothers are preparing for the day. One mother has already welcomed two new arrivals. She will keep the hatchlings in the nest for some time, bringing them food until they are old enough to forage for plants on their own.

LARGE COLONIES Nesting together in colonies meant that the eggs and hatchlings were better protected against predators. The mothers could take turns at keeping watch and seeing off intruders.

HARD TO KNOW Scientists disagree about whether dinosaur parents took care of their offspring. There is increasing evidence that many species nested together and enjoyed huddling or roosting for warmth and company, just as many birds do today. Some parents may also have spent time and effort preparing their hatchlings for adulthood.

The lethal claw

DEADLY CLAWS The enlarged second toe on each hind claw was a deadly weapon. It may have been used to slash at prey, or simply to pin a struggling victim down for the kill.

FEATHERS Unlike the larger raptors shown in the famous Jurassic Park films, real-life Velociraptors were about the size of a large dog and they lived in Mongolia, not North America. Scientists also think they had a fine coat of feather-like filaments. The Jurassic Park raptors are more similar to Deinonychus or Utahraptors.

LIFESTYLES Fossils don't leave many clues about how dinosaurs lived. We don't know if dinosaur mums taught their young hunting skills, but it's not unlikely.

HOME SCHOOLING

This Velociraptor mother has caught two small mammals and brought them back to her young so that they can practise their hunting skills. The shrew-like mammals are running for their lives but their chances of survival are slim!

VELOCIRAPTOR (Vel-OSS-ee-rap-tor)	LIVED	75–71 mya (Late Cretaceous) in Mongolia, northern China
	FAMILY	Dromeosauridae (see also Deinonychus)
	LENGTH	Up to 2 m (6.8 ft)
	WEIGHT	Up to 45 kg (100 lb)

HABITAT	Dry areas, with sand
DIET	Carnivore: hunted or scavenged small creatures such as reptiles, amphibians, insects, dinosaurs and mammals
KEY FACTS	Fast, smart, bipedal, feathered; carried a large, sickle-shaped claw on each hind foot

TOP NOTCH

Three Parasaurolophus gaze across the waters of a shallow sea. After a long drought there is no vegetation left in their usual feeding grounds. Will there be more on the other side? These large herbivores have an acute sense of smell and their noses tell them there is plenty of food just across the narrow sea. They are strong swimmers and are soon happily grazing.

WRONG HEADED At first, scientists thought that Parasaurolophus was amphibious (living between land and sea) and used its long head crest as a sort of snorkel to breathe underwater. They now know that they lived entirely on land, although they were powerful swimmers.

CRANIAL CREST

Short beak

The curved crests could grow to 1.8 metres (6 ft) long.

Hundreds of cheek teeth

DISPLAY The crests were probably used for display at mating time, to attract a partner. They were hollow and may also have been used to amplify calls.

PARASAUROLOPHUS
(PA-ra-SORE-oh-LOAF-us)

LIVED	77-73 mya (Late Cretaceous) in North America and possibly Asia
FAMILY	Hadrosauridae
LENGTH	Up to 11 m (36 ft)
HEIGHT	Up to 4.9 m (16 ft)
WEIGHT	Up to 1,650 kg (3,600 lb)
DIET	Herbivore: ate leaves, twigs and conifers
KEY FACTS	Large head crest, duck-billed; unusual tall narrow tails that may have been used to attract mates

HERDS Parasaurolophus lived on flood plains in large herds. They grazed on a wide variety of low-growing plants and bushes. They cropped the vegetation with their beaks and chewed it up using the teeth in their jaws that were continually replaced.

MAMMALS Placental mammals evolved during the Late Cretaceous. Like almost all modern mammals, these creatures had their babies at a late stage of development. They were all quite small, growing no larger than a modern rabbit, but they thrived and were ready to take over when the dinosaur age came to an end.

EARLY BIRDS

Enantiornithes all had well developed feathers and were strong fliers. Here you can see a large flock in the background.

A rowdy group of prehistoric birds sits on the backs of two Parasaurolophus dinosaurs, feasting on the bugs that live on their skins. These are the Enantiornithes, the largest group of birds during the Mesozoic Era. They all died out at the end of the Cretaceous.

A VARIED GROUP Enantiornithes was a large and varied group of birds that lived on every continent except Antarctica. More than 80 species have been named. Most of them were small, about the size of a modern sparrow or starling, but some grew to the size of a turkey or even larger. Their habitats and diets varied greatly, with some eating fish or bugs and others feasting on grain or hunting small mammals and reptiles.

The birds in the foreground are eating bugs off the dinosaurs' backs just as today's oxpeckers ride on large mammals like rhinos, giraffes and water buffalo feeding on the ticks, flies and other bugs on their skins.

TOOTHY BEAKS Enantiornithes had a wide range of body types. Unlike modern birds, they almost all had teeth. Some scientists have suggested that only the birds with no teeth survived the Cretaceous mass extinction. A toothless beak made it possible to crack and eat seeds. When food was scarce afer the asteroid hit, seeds from before the disaster were still available. Birds that could eat them survived.

ENANTIORNITHES
(En·an·tee·or·nee·thees)

LIVED	130–66 mya (Late Jurassic to Late Cretaceous) lived on every continent except Antarctica
CLADE	Enantiornithes
SIZE	Mainly small like sparrows and starlings, but some turkey-size
HABITAT	Lived in a wide range of habitats
DIET	Omnivores: ate insects, sap, berries, invertebrates and plants
KEY FACTS	Most common type of early bird; they had teeth; all died out at the end of the Cretaceous

RAPTORS AT BAY

Dinosaur eggs were a delicacy not to be missed! This Tarbosaurus — an Asian cousin of T-rex — is closing in on a nesting colony of Gigantoraptors and they react with terror at its approach. A fierce battle ensues, but luckily there are twelve adult raptors in the colony and they force the predator to retreat.

GIANT BIRD-LIKE DINOSAUR
Gigantoraptor is one of the largest bird-like dinosaurs ever discovered. It laid very large, elongated eggs, bigger than any other dinosaurs. It is known from just one, almost complete skeleton found in Mongolia in 2005.

HORNY BEAK

Gigantoraptor had a horny toothless beak, perfect for crushing tough plant matter and for tearing flesh.

GIGANTORAPTOR
(JIG-an-toe-rap-tor)

LIVED	83-70 mya (Late Cretaceous) in Mongolia
FAMILY	Caenagnathidae
LENGTH	Up to 8 m (26 ft)
HEIGHT	5 metres (16 ft)
WEIGHT	Up to 2,700 kg (6,000 lb)
DIET	Omnivore: fed on vegetation and small animals
KEY FACTS	Very large, bird-like dinosaur; may have had a full coat of feathers.

NOT REALLY RAPTORS Despite their name, Gigantoraptors were more closely related to Oviraptors than to true raptors such as Velociraptor. Gigantoraptors had very long, sharp claws but they lacked the sickle-shaped talons on their hind limbs that mark the true raptor.

BEHAVIOUR These huge creatures looked very like birds, so scientists think they may have behaved like birds too. For example, during courtship, mating pairs may have danced together in elaborate rituals. What a sight to see!

RICH PICKINGS

Dinosaur fossils are almost always found in sedimetary rocks which form when sand, silt, mud, and organic matter are compacted. All the dinosaurs shown here lived in one area of Alberta, Canada, known as the St. Mary River Formation.

REGALICERATOPS
(Re-gal-e-seh-rah-tops)

LIVED	68.5-67.5 mya (Late Cretaceous) in Alberta, Canada
FAMILY	Ceratopsidae
LENGTH	Up to 5 m (16.5 ft)
WEIGHT	Up to 2,000 kg (4,400 lb)
DIET	Herbivore: ate ferns, ginkgos and conifers
HABITAT	Swamps and floodplains
KEY FACTS	Aka Hellboy; very large; closely related to Triceratops; ornate neck frill and large nose horn

MONTANOCERATOPS

was a medium-size ceratopsid dinosaur with a large parrot-like beak. It had a huge head with a small frill (bony plate) on top. It was a primitive ceratopsid with claws on its feet instead of hooves and teeth in its upper jaws.

MONTANOCERATOPS
(Mon-tan-ah-ser-ah-tops)

LIVED	70 mya (Late Cretaceous) in North America	WEIGHT	500 kg (900 lb)
FAMILY	Ceratopsidae	DIET	Herbivore: ate ferns, ginkgos and conifers
LENGTH	Up to 3 m (10 ft)	HABITAT	Swamps and floodplains
HEIGHT	1 m (3.3 ft)	KEY FACTS	Primitive ceratopsid; claws instead of hooves; parrot-like beak

REGALICERATOPS

This ceratopsid dinosaur's name means "royal horned face," but it is also known as Hellboy. It was about the size of a big SUV and had a large, ornate neck frill and three horns on its face, so both names suit it very well.

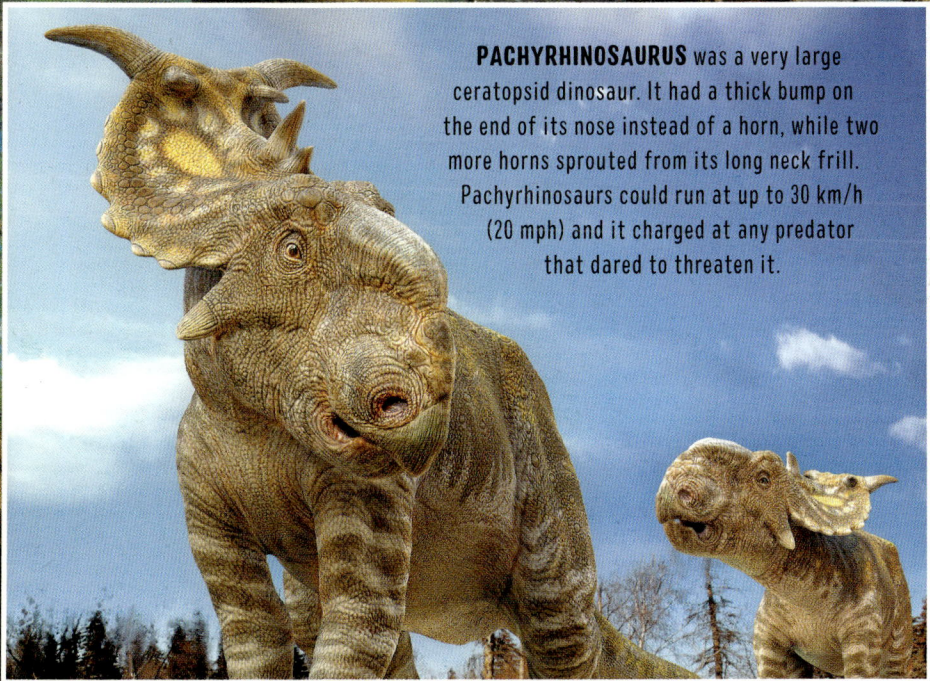

PACHYRHINOSAURUS was a very large ceratopsid dinosaur. It had a thick bump on the end of its nose instead of a horn, while two more horns sprouted from its long neck frill. Pachyrhinosaurs could run at up to 30 km/h (20 mph) and it charged at any predator that dared to threaten it.

PACHYRHINOSAURUS (PAK-ee-rye-no-SORE-us)

LIVED	76-71 mya (Late Cretaceous) in North America
FAMILY	Ceratopsidae
LENGTH	Up to 8 m (26 ft)
WEIGHT	Up to 3,600 kg (7,200 lb)
DIET	Herbivore: ate ferns, ginkgos and conifers
HABITAT	Swamps and floodplains
KEY FACTS	Large ceratopsid; could run fast for its size; lump on its nose instead of a horn

HUNTERS IN THE SKY

Thalassodromeus soars above the sea, powered along by its huge, membraneous wings. Like a modern bird of prey, it surveys the ground below, looking for victims. However, it doesn't dive down to scoop up fish or land reptiles. Instead it lands, and stalks its prey on foot.

CRETACEOUS PTEROSAURS

By Cretaceous times most pterosaurs were pterodactyloids. They had narrow wings, short tails and long necks with large heads. Many had no teeth in their horny beaks. They hunted on the ground, walking on all fours in an upright position.

Thalassodromeus had a crest on the back of its head that was three times longer than the rest of its skull. One of the largest known, it was crisscrossed with blood vessels and may have been used to regulate body temperature. It may also have been used for display, in order to attract a mate.

QUETZALCOATLUS
(Kwet-sal-co-AT-lus)

WINGSPAN	33–39 feet
WEIGHT	Disputed, but probably around 550 pounds
DIET	Carnivore: ate small dinosaurs, other reptiles and early mammals
LIVED	71–66 mya (Late Cretaceous) in North America
KEY FACTS	One of the largest pterosaurs, about the size of a light aircraft
FAMILY	Azhdarchidae

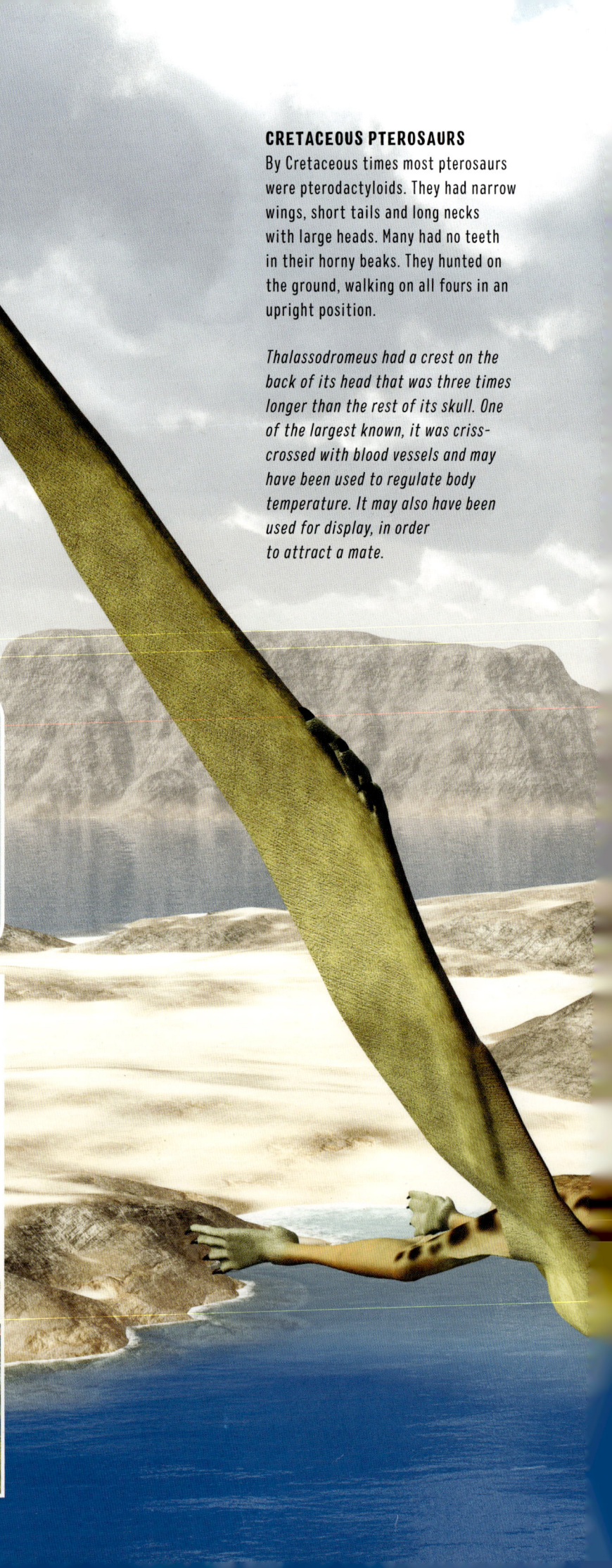

FLIGHT Some scientists have suggested that Quetzalcoatlus was too heavy to fly. But most think that it could vault into the air using its powerful limbs, or jump from a clifftop. Once airborne, it could soar and glide at speeds of up to 90 km/h (56 mph).

At first, palaeontologists thought that Quetzalcoatlus fed on fish by skimming over the surface of the sea like many smaller pterosaurs. But Quetzalcoatlus was far too big to hunt this way. It hunted on the ground, capturing prey with its huge beak.

THALASSODROMEUS
(Thah-LASS-oh-DRO-me-us)

LIVED	110–100 mya (Early Cretaceous) in Brazil
FAMILY	Thalassodromidae
WINGSPAN	4–5 m (13–17 ft)
WEIGHT	Unknown
HABITAT	Wetlands and coastal regions
DIET	Carnivore: ate small reptiles and other animals, stalked them on the ground
KEY FACTS	Large pterosaur; huge ornate skull crest; toothless jaws; known only from pieces of broken skull

HUNTING METHODS The eyes of the Elasmosaurus were positioned on the top of its head, and scientists believe that it swam along the ocean floor beneath unsuspecting prey before suddenly ambushing them from below. It may also have side-swiped large prey with its projecting teeth before swallowing them whole.

SEA MONSTERS

Elasmosaurus is feeling peckish as it cruises along the shallow sea floor, its keen eyes peeled for a fishy morsel. The huge reptile has been underwater for over 10 minutes now and will soon have to surface for air. Then suddenly, it spies a large squid just above its head, and immediately prepares to strike!

NORTH AMERICA SUBMERGED For most of the Cretaceous much of central North America was covered by shallow seas. Elasmosaurus was just one of many marine reptiles that lived there. Others included ichthyosaurs, nothosaurs, placodonts and mosasaurs.

ONE OF MANY Elasmosaurus was one of the largest members of a group of marine reptiles called plesiosaurs that lived from the Late Triassic until the end of the dinosaur era. Some people believe that the Loch Ness Monster in Scotland really exists and that it is a type of plesiosaur.

LONG NECK Elasmosaurus had an immensely elongated neck that took up at least half of its entire body length. Its head was tiny in comparison. When palaeontologists first tried to reconstruct Elasmosaurus, they put its head at the wrong end!

ELASMOSAURUS
(Ee-LAZZ-mo-SORE-rus)

LIVED	80 mya (Late Cretaceous) in seas worldwide
FAMILY	Elasmosauridae
LENGTH	Up to 15 m (50 ft)
WEIGHT	About 2,750 kg (6,000 lb)

HABITAT	Shallow seas
DIET	Carnivore: ate fish and marine invertebrates
KEY FACTS	Very long neck, tiny head; among the largest plesiosaurs; probably gave birth to live young

SMALL FRILLS

A big Udanoceratops lumbers into the clearing in search of food. It finds plenty of the low-growing ferns and cycads it likes to eat and tucks in. Using its sharp, sturdy beak it shears off parts of the tough plants and chomps them to a pulp with the teeth in the back of its huge jaws before swallowing.

NO HORNS Despite its name, which means "horned face from Udan," this distant relative of Triceratops did not have any horns on its face. Its head frill was also quite small. It is one of a number of ceratopsids that had small facial horns and frills or none at all.

PARROT BEAK Udanoceratops had a large toothless beak which it used to grasp and bite off the tough vegetation that grew in its desert habitat. The teeth inside its mouth were used to shear and crush the food before swallowing.

DEFENSIVE WEAPONS Udanoceratops could not move very quickly so it relied on its strong sense of smell to avoid predators. When faced with a hungry carnivore, it used its powerful jaws and large horny beak to inflict devastating bites. Male Udanoceratops also used their beaks when fighting among themselves for mating rights.

DEEP JAWS, HEAVY SKULL

Udanoceratops is known mainly from a single large, almost-intact skull. Only parts of the rest of its body have been found. Its large nostrils suggest that it had an excellent sense of smell which it used to find food and to detect predators before they got too close.

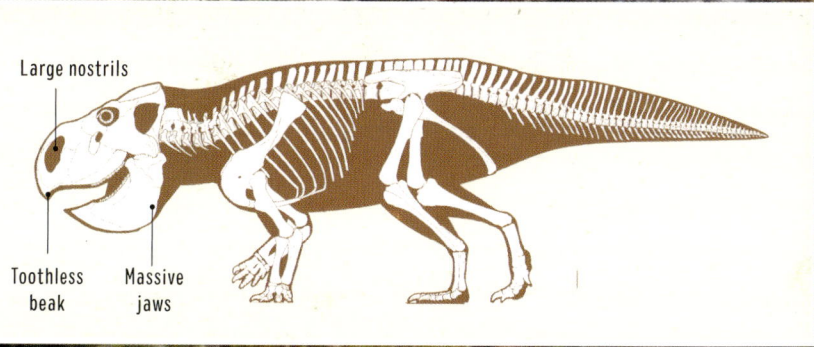

Large nostrils

Toothless beak

Massive jaws

UDANOCERATOPS (Oo-DAHN-oh-serra-tops)	LIVED	81–75 mya (Late Cretaceous) in Mongolia	WEIGHT	Up to 700 kg (1500 lb)
	FAMILY	Leptoceratopsidae	DIET	Herbivore: ate tough vegetation
	LENGTH	Up to 4 m (13 ft)	HABITAT:	Dry, desert-like
	HEIGHT	Up to 1 m (3.3 ft)	KEY FACTS	Large ceratopsid with no horns and only a small frill; massive jaws

COURTSHIP BELLOWS

The Therizinosaurus's whole body shakes with the effort as he lets out a string of ear-splitting roars. Small mammals scuttle to safety and birds flutter from the trees. It's springtime and this colossal, bizarre-looking creature is searching for a mate. With each roar he extends his long, fearsome claws. Soon enough, he hears an answering bellow from just beyond the hill.

CLAWSOME!

Therizinosaurus grew claws up to one metre (3.2 ft) long! Their purpose is unknown, although they may have been used for defence or display at mating time. Some think they were useful to reach up high in the trees and pull down juicy leaves.

A STRANGE LOOKING DINOSAUR

Therizinosaurus was as big as a large T-rex. Being tall meant it could reach leaves higher up in the trees. It moved on its hind legs and had very long arms and an unusually large stomach. Scientists now have almost complete skeletons of this bizarre creature to study. They are amazed by its unique appearance.

THERIZINOSAURUS
(TERRY-zin-oh-SORE-us)

LIVED	100-66 mya (Late Cretaceous) in Asia and North America
FAMILY	Therizinosauridae
LENGTH	Up to 10 m (33 ft)
HEIGHT	7 m (23 ft)
WEIGHT	Up to 5,000 kg (11,000 lb)
Habitat	Woodlands
DIET	Herbivore / Omnivore: mainly ate plants, but may also have eaten small animals and insects
KEY FACTS	Tall, with very long arms and claws; bizarre appearance

DISCOVERY Therizinosaurus remains were first discovered in 1948 and were declared to be part of a giant turtle. It took another 25 years before scientists correctly identified them as belonging to a theropod dinosaur.

NESTS AND EGGS

A well-preserved Therizinosaurus nesting colony was found in the Gobi Desert, in Mongolia. Therizinosaurus mothers were too big and heavy to incubate their eggs as they would have crushed them. Instead, they laid their eggs in nests then covered them with sand or vegetation to keep them safe and warm until they hatched.

A few fossilised eggs have been found with tiny embryos inside. Here you can see a baby Therizonosaurus in its egg; its long claws are already well developed.

FEATHERS Some Therizinosaurus fossils have shown feather-like filaments growing on the chest, forelimbs and hind limbs, but we don't know if these creatures had a complete covering of feathers.

THE LAST DAY

Many of the best-known dinosaurs were alive on the day the asteroid hit: Triceratops, T-rex, Anklyosaurus and many others were all unaware that their long reign was about to end!

CRETACEOUS TYRANTS T-rex was just one member of a group of tyrannosaurs that lived from the Late Jurassic until the end of the dinosaur age. They were all large, fierce predators.

DAWN TERROR

T-rex had a mouthful of teeth up to 20 cm (8 in) long. Its jaw grip was three times that of a modern lion and it had a keen sense of smell to track down its victims.

With a brood of hungry youngsters to feed, this female T-rex has a lot on her plate! Working alone in the dawn light, she tracks an Edmontosaurus and pounces. One bite with her powerful jaws is enough. The herbivore doesn't stand a chance. The T-rex family feasts on its carcass before resting through the heat of the day.

TYRANNOSAURUS REX
(TIE-ran-oh-SORE-us rex)

LIVED	70-66 mya (Late Cretaceous) in North America
FAMILY	Tyrannosauridae
LENGTH	Up to 14 m (46 ft)
HEIGHT	6.5 m (21 ft)
WEIGHT	Up to 7,000 kg (15,000 lb)
DIET	Carnivore: hunted other dinosaurs, including large herbivores like Edmontosaurus
KEY FACTS	Large, powerful predator; very small forelimbs; active hunter and scavenger

BIGGEST CARNIVORE The aptly named "King of the tyrant lizards" was the largest predator in North America. T-rex used its sharp, serrated teeth and powerful jaws to tear the flesh off its victims, throwing back its head to toss the meat down its throat.

CANNIBALISM T-rex was a scavenger as well as an active hunter. Fossils show that these fearsome creatures sometimes hunted down other predators, even of their own species.

ENJOYING THE SHADE

A large Deinocheirus sits comfortably in the cool forest after a busy morning spent gobbling up plants and fish in the river nearby. Huge and truly bizarre-looking, this dinosaur has big, clawed hands, a hump similar to a camel and beak like a duck!

PREDATORS Deinocheirus lived alongside fierce predators like Tarbosaurus, an Asian member of the Tyrannosaur family that was only slightly smaller than T-rex. Deinocheirus's large size would have discouraged most smaller predators, but it was bulky and slow-moving and was probably hunted by big predators.

A MIXED DIET Fossils reveal that Deinocheirus dined on both plants and animals. Gastroliths, or small stomach stones, have been found among the fossils. The toothless Deinocheirus swallowed the stones to help grind up tough plant material in its gizzards. Fish bones and scales have also been found in its fossilised stomach, showing that it caught fish in the local lakes and streams.

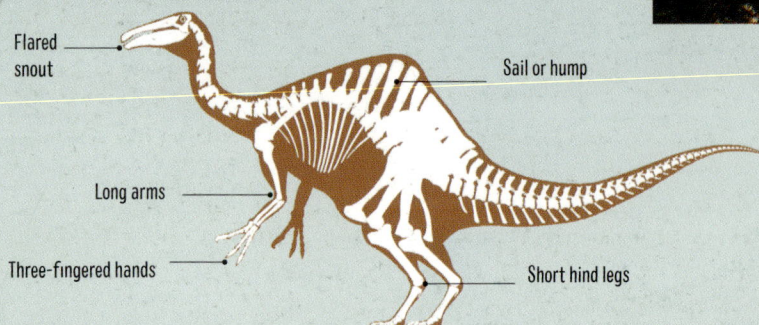

Flared snout

Sail or hump

Long arms

Three-fingered hands

Short hind legs

MASSIVE ARMS For a long time Deinocheirus was known only by the fossils of two huge arms. The rest of its body remained a mystery until two more complete skeletons were discovered in 2014. They showed that it had a hump or sail on its back, short hind legs, feathers, hollow bones and a duck-like beak.

Deinocheirus
(DIE-no-KAI-russ)

LIVED	100-66 mya (Late Cretaceous) in Mongolia
FAMILY	Deinocheiridae
LENGTH	Up to 11 m (36 ft)
WEIGHT	About 6,500 kg (14,300 lb)

HABITAT	Floodplains with mudflats, rivers and shallow lakes
DIET	Omnivore: ate plants, insects and small animals, including fish
KEY FACTS	Huge, bizarre-looking dinosaur with feathers, a hump and large arms

ARMOURED AND DANGEROUS

A group of Ankylosaurus lumber down to the lakeside to drink in the cool evening breeze. Built like tanks, they fear no one. Their bodies are entirely covered in bony armour made up of hundreds of plates and spikes. On their tails, they carry a lethal bony club. Other herbivores take care not to disturb them and even the crocodile-like predators in the water keep their distance.

ANKYLOSAURUS
(ANK-ill-oh-SORE-us)

LIVED	70-66 mya (Late Cretaceous) in North America
FAMILY	Ankylosauridae
LENGTH	Up to 10 m (33 ft)
WEIGHT	Up to 8,000 kg (17,500 lb)

HABITAT	Warm tropical and sub-tropical forests
DIET	Herbivore: ate ferns and low-growing plants
KEY FACTS	Colossal, with a full coat of body armour and clubbed tail; a famous dinosaur known from fossil fragments only

TAIL CLUB Ankylosaurus was armed with a hefty tail club made of solid bone. Thick tendons ran down to the base of the tail where powerful muscles were attached to the hips. This allowed the Ankylosaurus to swing its tail from side to side with great force – it was a fearsome weapon!

DON'T MESS WITH ME!

It is mating season in the Cretaceous woodlands and the male Triceratops are stamping and roaring and tussling one another with their long horns. Each one hopes to impress the females and earn mating rights. Even the pouring rain does not put them off!

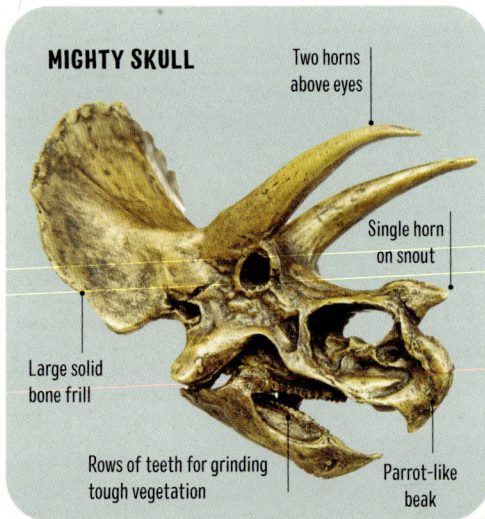

MIGHTY SKULL

Two horns above eyes

Single horn on snout

Large solid bone frill

Rows of teeth for grinding tough vegetation

Parrot-like beak

COLOSSAL BEAST As long as two cars and weighing as much as two elephants, Triceratops was a massive creature. Yet despite its size and fearsome appearance, it was a herbivore and used its impressive horns and skull for defence and to signal other Triceratops, especially in the mating season.

TRICERATOPS
(Tri-SER-a-tops)

LIVED	68-66 mya (Late Cretaceous) in North America
FAMILY	Ceratopsidae
LENGTH	Up to 9 m (30 ft)
WEIGHT	8,000 kg (17,500 lb)
HABITAT	Dry, forested areas and plains
DIET	Herbivore: low-growing plants such as palms, cycads and ferns
KEY FACTS	Huge skull made up one-third of body; huge frill and horns; had up to 800 cheek teeth

DID THEY EVER FIGHT T-REX? Every film and video game shows Triceratops battling a T-rex. The two dinosaurs lived in close proximity and T-rex almost certainly hunted Triceratops. But an adult Triceratops was large and well armed, so T-rex probably targeted young or sick animals.

HEAD BUTTERS!

Under the watchful eye of their mother, two juvenile Pachycephalosaurus lower their heads and charge towards one another at breakneck speed. The young dinosaurs are practising the head-butting skills they will use as adults to win mating rights and defend themselves. Luckily they have already developed a dome of solid bone on their skulls!

FAST AND AGILE Moving on its sturdy hind legs, Pachycephalosaurus could run fast. In fact, fleeing was probably its best line of defence if threatened by any of the many predatory dinosaurs such as T-rex or Albertosaurus that also lived on the North American floodplains.

PACHYCEPHALOSAURUS
(PACK-ee-sef-al-low-SORE-us)

LIVED	72-66 mya (Late Cretaceous) in North America
FAMILY	Pachycephalosauridae
LENGTH	Up to 4.5 m (14.8 ft)
WEIGHT	Up to 435 kg (950 lb)
HABITAT	Floodplains, forests and green areas
DIET	Omnivore: ate leaves, seeds and fruits; may also have eaten insects and small animals
KEY FACTS	Bony, domed head; tiny brain; huge eyes; excellent sense of smell

BONEHEAD The top of the skull was a dome of solid bone up to 40 cm (16 in) thick.

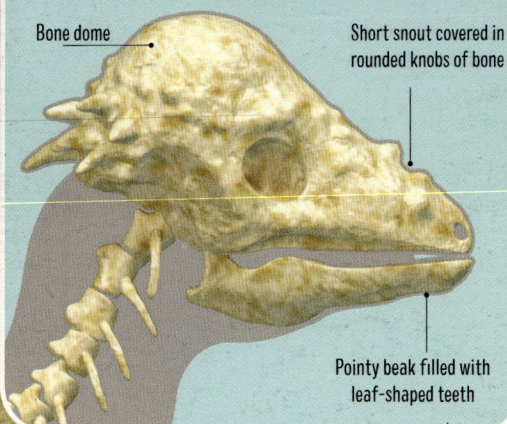

Bone dome

Short snout covered in rounded knobs of bone

Pointy beak filled with leaf-shaped teeth

COUSINS There were several closely related species of Pachycephalosaurs. They all had thick, bony skulls although some were flat or wedge-shaped rather than domed. They all had sturdy bodies and a stiff heavy tail, which was held out behind for balance.

PEACEFUL GRAZERS

A herd of Edmontosaurus grazes peacefully in the tropical heat. The only sounds are insects buzzing and the grinding of teeth as the big herbivores chew the tough conifer and fern leaves. They need to eat almost constantly just to survive. But not everyone is eating: one of the group keeps a vigilant watch out for predators.

DIFFICULT NEIGHBOURS
Edmontosaurus lived in the same habitat as Tyrannosaurus rex. Fossils show that some duckbills escaped a Tyrannosaur attack, perhaps by running away. Edmontosaurus could move at 45 km/h (28 mph) over short distances!

ENDLESS ROWS OF TEETH Edmontosaurus had three rows of 60 teeth up and down each side of its immense jaws. That's a total of 720 teeth! An adult human has 32. If a tooth fell out a new one grew quickly in its place.

SOCIAL ANIMALS Edmontosaurus lived in groups. They could move on two legs or four but seemed to have spent most of their time on their hind legs. Unlike many duckbills, Edmontosaurs did not have a bony crest on its head.

INFLATABLE NOSE FLAP

Edmontosaurus had a flap of skin on its nose that it could inflate and use to amplify its loud calls. The flap may also have been used to impress partners during the mating season.

FLOWERS AND INSECTS

Flowering plants, such as magnolias, palms and laurels, first grew in the Cretaceous. Insects had been around for much longer. The earliest insects appeared at least 150 million years before the dinosaurs.

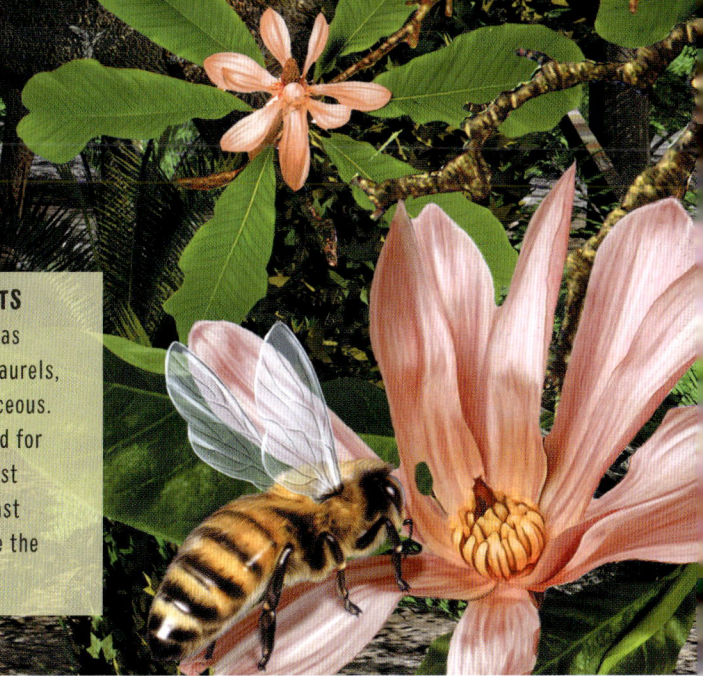

EDMONTOSAURUS
(Ed-MON-toe-SORE-us)

LIVED	73-66 mya (Late Cretaceous) in North America
FAMILY	Hadrosauridae
LENGTH	Up to 15 m (49 ft)
WEIGHT	9,000 kg (20,000 lb)

HABITAT	Coastal plains with swamps, tropical conifer forests and ferns
DIET	Herbivore: ate conifer and broadleaf trees, small seeds and fruits
KEY FACTS	Thick tough skin, bipedal (moving on hind legs), capable of bursts of speed despite large size

FEARLESS PREDATORS

Blood-curdling grunts and screams echo across the valley as a pack of vicious Dakotaraptors attack an elderly T-rex. These stealthy raptors stalked their prey, waiting for the right moment to ambush them. Their attacks were well-planned, quick and brutal.

FEATHERS Dakotaraptor was covered in feathers and its wings were similar to those of modern birds. It was too heavy to fly so the wings were probably used to pin down prey or to impress rivals during courtship displays. They may also have been used to shelter and protect their young.

SOCIAL ANIMALS Dakotaraptors were social animals that lived together in small family packs. They had large brains and excellent eyesight and could run at 65 km/h (40 mph). Their long legs and slender build meant that they could chase prey over long distances.

HUNTING IN PACKS Dakotaraptor was one of the few dinosaurs brave enough to take on a fully grown T-rex. These medium-size predators were armed with the raptor's usual sickle-shaped claw on their second toes which they used to slash victims. They could hunt small and medium prey on their own, but by working together in packs they could bring down large animals like Triceratops or T-rex.

WHO WILL WIN? The old T-rex will eventually succumb, but not without inflicting some serious wounds on its attackers.

DAKOTARAPTOR (Dak-o-ta-rap-tur)	LIVED	70-66 mya (Late Cretaceous) in North America	HABITAT	Coastal plains with woodlands, ponds and swamps
	FAMILY	Dromaeosauridae	DIET	Carnivorous: ate other dinosaurs and reptiles of all sizes
	LENGTH	Up to 6 m (20 ft)	KEY FACTS	Large feathered raptors; aggressive hunters; lived at the end of the dinosaur age with T-rex, Triceratops and many other famous dinosaurs
	HEIGHT	Up to 2 m (6.5 ft)		
	WEIGHT	Up to 350 kg (770 lb)		

ARMOURED TITANS

The Earth literally shakes as a herd of colossal Alamosaurus ambles across the wooded plains of what is now the southern United States. These are the largest dinosaurs that ever walked on American soil. They lived at the end of the Cretaceous, about 30 million years after most of the other giant sauropods had become extinct.

Alamosaurus could rear up on its hind legs to reach succulent leaves in the treetops.

GRANDSTAND VIEW OF THE LAST DAY Fossils for these dinosaurs have been found in different parts of the American south, including Utah, New Mexico and Texas. They show that Alamosaurus was alive when the asteroid hit. Given their location, they would have had a grandstand view of its arrival and been among the first to suffer the consequences.

FAST GROWTH Alamosaurus eggs were about the size of a basketball. Juveniles grew fast, probably adding up to 30 pounds a day to their bodyweight during spurts of growth. They reached full size at about eight or nine years of age and lived for at least 50 years.

A GIANT CREATURE The average Alamosaurus body was wider than a modern family car is long! Their legs were very sturdy and column-like to carry their heavy bodies. They had to eat constantly to maintain their weight.

SPIKES AND ARMOUR Alamosaurus was at least partly covered by boby armour. It also had a row of spikes running down its neck and back.

ALAMOSAURUS
(A-luh-muh-SORE-us)

LIVED	70-66 mya (Late Cretaceous) in North America
FAMILY	Saltasauridae
LENGTH	Up to 30 m (98 ft)
WEIGHT	Up to 80,000 kg (176,000 lb)

HEIGHT	Up to 8.4 m (27.5 ft)
HABITAT	Semi-arid inland plains
DIET	Herbivore: conifer and broadleaf trees, small seeds and fruits
KEY FACTS	Thick tough skin, bipedal (moving on hind legs), capable of bursts of speed despite large size

FIERCE CANNIBALS

A Majungasaurus trots across the hot sands of what is now Madagascar. This apex predator is famished and it will stop at nothing to fill its stomach, even if it means attacking members of its own kind. Majungasaurus is one of the few dinosaurs where there is direct evidence of cannibalism.

TOP HUNTER Majungasaurus was the largest predator in its environment. It usually hunted other dinosaurs, especially sauropods like the Rapetosaurus. It had a short broad snout, a mouth full of small, strong teeth and powerful jaws that could deliver a devastating bite. There is evidence that it ate its own species in the form of bite marks in fossilised Majungasaurus' bones that could only have been made by their own specialised and recognisable teeth.

MADAGASCAR Today the island of Madagascar lies off the coast of Africa but during most of the Mesozoic it was connected to India. Fossils are quite different from those in Africa, and the dinosaurs excavated there have more in common with those in India. There are also some unique species that have only been found in Madagascar.

APPEARANCE Majungasaurus had rough skin with standout scales and osteoderms. On top of its head it had a single rounded horn. Majungasaurus was a bipedal predator with a short snout. Its forelimbs were tiny, even smaller than those of T-rex.

MAJUNGASAURUS
(Ma-JUNG-ah-SORE-us)

LIVED	70-66 mya (Late Cretaceous) in Madagascar
FAMILY	Abelisauridae
LENGTH	Up to 7 m (23 ft)
WEIGHT	Up to 1,100 kg (2,400 lb)
HABITAT	Warm coastal plains with rivers
DIET	Carnivore: other dinosaurs, even of its own species
KEY FACTS	Large predatory dinosaur; one of only a handful of species that were known cannibals

HUNTING TITANS

Here we can see two daring Alioramus hunting a herd of Olorotitans. It's a bold move and their plan - which seems to be working - is to frighten the large duck-billed herbivores, panicking them into flight, so that they will leave any young, sick or elderly members of the herd unattended.

OLOROTITAN
(Ol-lo-ro-TIE-ten)

LIVED	70-66 mya (Late Cretaceous) in Far Eastern Russia
FAMILY	Hadrosauridae
LENGTH	Up to 12 m (39 ft)
HEIGHT	Up to 4 m (13 ft)
WEIGHT	Up to 4,500 kg (10,000 lb)
DIET	Herbivore: plants and leaves
HABITAT	Woodlands and marshes
KEY FACTS	A big duck-billed dinosaur with a very large crest

CRESTS Olorotitan had a large, fan-shaped crest on its head. It was connected to its nasal cavity, so may have increased the animal's sense of smell. It could also have been used for vocalisation (calls). If it was brightly colored, it may have been used for recognition or to attract a mate during the mating season.

A LARGE HADROSAUR Olorotitan was a very large duck-billed dinosaur. It was related to North American species like Parasaurolophus (see pages 116-117). It was bipedal (moved on two legs) although it often dropped onto four legs to feed or rest. Olorotitan had strong, slender legs and could run fast. Like all hadrosaurs, its beak was broad, shaped like a modern duck's bill and filled with batteries of teeth.

A SLENDER TYRANNOSAUR

Alioramus relied on speed and agility to hunt. It didn't have the same bone-crushing power in its jaws of other Tryannosaurs and was only about half the size of its larger American cousin, T-rex. It usually hunted smaller prey, but may have attacked large herbivores as part of a pack.

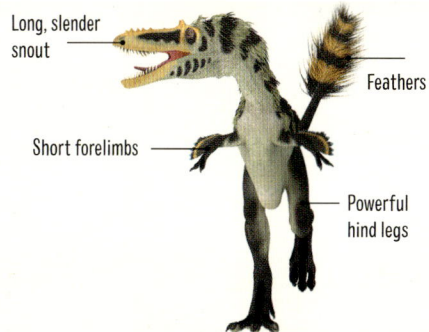

Long, slender snout

Feathers

Short forelimbs

Powerful hind legs

ALIORAMUS
(AL-ee-oh-RAY-mus)

LIVED	72–66 mya (Late Jurassic) in Mongolia and Russia	
FAMILY	Tyrannosauridae	
LENGTH	Up to 6 m (20ft)	
WEIGHT	Up to 700 kg (1500 lb)	

DIET	Carnivore: hunted smaller dinosaurs and other reptiles
HABITAT	Wet humid floodplains and pine forests
KEY FACTS	Medium-sized fast predator; feather covering; hunted small to medium prey

THE LAST DAY

The dinosaurs lived for 180 million years until, about 66 million years ago, they suddenly disappeared from the fossil record. Most scientists now believe that they died out because an asteroid at least 10 km (6 miles) wide and travelling at about 77,000 km/h (48,000 mph) slammed into the Earth causing a mass extinction that wiped out not just the dinosaurs, but three-quarters of all living things.

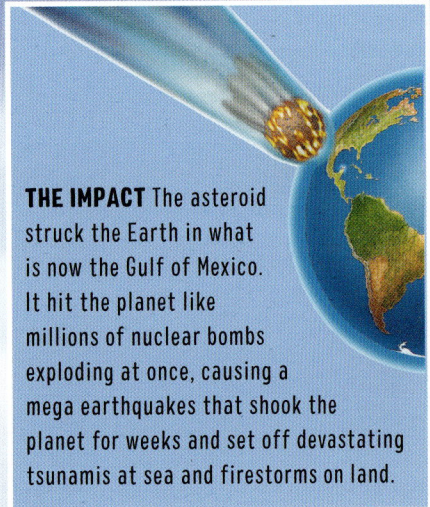

THE IMPACT The asteroid struck the Earth in what is now the Gulf of Mexico. It hit the planet like millions of nuclear bombs exploding at once, causing a mega earthquakes that shook the planet for weeks and set off devastating tsunamis at sea and firestorms on land.

The dinosaurs in current-day North and South America were closest to the impact zone. Many of them would have died within minutes of the asteroid strike.

OTHER THEORIES Some scientists think that Earth was experiencing changes that made life harder before the asteroid hit. They claim that dinosaur numbers were already in decline. A million years of intense volcanic activity in India had thrown ashes and dust into the skies, creating greenhouse conditions which led to climate change. At the same time, continents were drifting apart, creating bigger oceans and less land. According to this point of view, the asteroid was just the final blow.

T-rex, Triceratops and duckbills like the ones shown here were all living in North America when the asteroid hit.

THE EVIDENCE We know that there was a huge asteroid strike 66 million years ago because scientists have found a layer of metal called iridium in the Earth's crust that dates to that time. Iridium is rare on Earth but is plentiful in asteroids. Scientists have also found the impact crater on the coast of the Yucatan Peninsula, in Mexico.

THE AFTERMATH

The fallout from the asteroid strike continued for a long time. The dust and smoke hurled into the atmosphere blocked out the Sun for several years. Starved of light, plants could not grow and the animals that fed on them died of hunger. The Earth's entire ecosystem collapsed and only a small number of creatures survived.

In the minutes following impact a hailstorm of tiny glass beads rained down on North America. Palaeontologists have found layers of them at Hell Creek and other dinosaur-rich fossil sites.

DARK TIMES For up to two years after the impact the Earth was wrapped in a blanket of soot and dust. In the darkness, plants could not carry out photosynthesis and the animals that ate them died out.

THE VICTIMS

About three-quarters of all the animals on Earth died out at the end of the Cretaceous. In addition to the non-avian (non-bird) dinosaurs, all the pterosaurs became extinct, as well as many Mesozoic birds. In the seas, plesiosaurs and mosasaurs were killed off, alongside many teleost fish, sharks and molluscs. A great many plants were also lost.

HEAT SURGE For several hours after impact, the Earth was bathed in an intense rush of heat caused by debris re-entering the atmosphere. Plants caught fire and animals were burnt. On land, much of Cretaceous life was wiped out within hours.

BIRDS Avian dinosaurs, also known as birds, not only survived the impact, they flourished. Today, there are more than 10,000 different species of birds.

THE SURVIVORS
Fortunately a number of plants and animals did survive the calamity and were soon able to replenish life on Earth. Some species of crocodiles, lizards, snakes, frogs, salamanders, turtles, fish and mammals all made it through. A large number of flowering plants survived and flourished as better conditions returned.

THE AGE OF MAMMALS About 90 per cent of mammals died out. However, they soon recovered and the Cenozoic Era that began 66 million years ago is known as the Age of Mammals.

INDEX

ACKNOWLEDGMENTS

The Publisher would like to thank the following illustrators and picture archives.

Shutterstock
Pages 2-3, 6-7, 8-9, 12-13, 14-15, 16-17, 24-25, 30-31, 36-37, 38-39, 54-55, 56-57, 60-61, 62-63, 74-75, 76, 93, 96-97, 98-99, 100-101, 108-109, 110-111, 116-117, 120-121, 123, 124-125, 126-127, 130-131, 132-133, 134-135, 136-137, 144-145, 146-147, 148-149, 150-151, 156-157

Leonello Calvetti and Luca Massini
Pages 1, 4-5, 10-11, 28-29, 46-47, 50-51, 70-71, 72-73, 78-79, 80-81, 82-83, 84-85, 90-91, 92-93, 94-95, 102-103, 104-105, 112-113, 114-115, 138-139, 140-141, 142-143, 158

SCIENCE PHOTO LIBRARY
Pages 18-19, 32-33, 34-35, 40-41, 48-49, 52-53, 58-59, 64-65, 66-67, 76-77, 86-87, 88-89, 106-107, 118-119, 122-123, 128-129, 152-153, 154-155

Ivan Stalio
Pages 19, 20-21, 26-27, 28, 41, 42-43, 44-45, 48, 55, 71, 87, 145

Andrey Atuchin
Pages 22-23, 68-69

Daniel Hamiliton
Pages 130, 131

A special thanks to Andrea Dué